FIND ME
THE MONEY

FIND ME
THE MONEY

*Take Control, Uncover the Truth, and
Win the Money You Deserve
in Your Divorce*

TRACY COENEN

ethos
collective

Published by Ethos Collective™
PO Box 43, Powell, OH 43065
www.ethoscollective.vip

Library of Congress Control Number: 2023904341
Paperback: 978-1-63680-137-7
Hardcover: 978-1-63680-138-4
Ebook: 978-1-63680-139-1

Available in hardcover, softcover, e-book, and audiobook.

DEDICATION

This is a reminder to every woman facing uncertainty and divorce—no, scratch that. It's not a reminder at all.

It is encouragement. Encouragement to be brave, to be tenacious, and to fight to win what you deserve during your divorce.

May you find your strength and take back your power.

And may this book inspire you to become exactly who you were always meant to be:

Gloriously happy and free.

CONTENTS

PART THREE: FUTURE

INTRODUCTION

NOBODY PLANS FOR THIS: JACKIE'S STORY

A million thoughts ran through her mind as she let the word sink in: *Divorce.*

How could he throw away fourteen years for a fling?

That morning had started like every other. Jackie got the kids ready for school while Derrick got ready for work. They never chatted before he left. Some days she didn't even hear him walk out the door.

But this morning, Derrick had lingered over his coffee and offered to take their three children to school. When she heard him come back, Jackie knew something was wrong. The coffee he poured remained untouched as he listed the reasons he needed to leave. She begged him to go to counseling, but he wasn't interested.

"She's been there for me for the last three years. It's time for me to be there for her."

Was that supposed to be a good reason for abandoning his family?

He went on and on about everything Jackie had done wrong. "You know you drove me to it, Jackie."

I should have seen it coming. Were all those out-of-town trips actually work-related?

He made sure she knew that his paycheck was his. The retirement account was his. He earned all of it. He paid for the house. He paid for the cars. He wasn't going to go broke paying for her to sit at home all day.

Does he really think I don't earn my keep running this household and raising these kids while he works late most nights? Does he even consider that giving up my career was hard, but I thought we were in this together for the good of our family?

Derrick always acted and talked like they were a team and the family finances were really for the family. But now his words seem so cold. He sounds so selfish.

Of course he's selfish. He's been having an affair for three years. Three years. Or so he says. I wonder how long it has really been going on.

Derrick picked up the suitcase and headed for the door.

When did he pack that?

For the rest of the day, Jackie tried to wrap her brain around everything Derrick had said. It just didn't feel real.

Jackie knew she needed to pull herself together before she picked up her kids from school, but her husband's assurance that she wouldn't see a penny of his retirement savings account made her question her decision to leave her marketing career to be a stay-at-home mom. After ten years, with so many technological advances, she wondered if she'd be able to keep up.

Tears welled in her eyes as she thought about starting at the bottom again at thirty-seven.

How will I make ends meet? What if the courts believe it was my fault? Will I make enough to cover the mortgage, or will we have to move? I am going to struggle for the rest of my life, and I'll probably never be able to retire, thanks to his bad choices. This isn't what we planned. This isn't fair to the kids.

She couldn't stop the flurry of emotions—worry, anger, shock, shame. She didn't even know how much money they had or where the money was. Derrick took care of all the finances.

Is that because he spends all our extra money on the other woman? Why didn't I pay more attention?

Jackie couldn't remember the last time she actually looked at a bank statement. And credit cards? She had two she regularly used, and Derrick told her which types of things went on each. No, the groceries go on *that* one. Gas goes on *this* one. It all felt so controlling now that she started thinking about it.

He talked about having investments and always said they were "fine" financially.

What did that mean? How much do we have? Where are these investments? Would I even know if he had hidden some stocks away in a secret account? Of course, I wouldn't. I haven't been watching the money because I had no reason to suspect anything was wrong.

Jackie had put so much trust in her husband, but how well did she know him? Would he give her a fair share of their assets?

Wait. Give? Don't we both own these things? Isn't everything half mine too? Why does he get to lay claim to all of it and then decide if he wants to "give" some to me?

The thoughts were coming faster than Jackie could process them. She could feel the panic growing. This can't really be happening. All of their plans for their family. The financial security "they" were building as Derrick stayed late at work so often. Or so he said. And now Jackie had to worry whether the bills would be paid.

Will the kids be able to stay in this school district, or will I have to move somewhere more affordable? How long will this feeling of betrayal haunt me?

Overwhelmed and unsure of her future, Jackie had no idea where to turn.

* * *

Jackie is a composite of many wonderful people I've served over the past twenty-five years. I have the privilege of helping men and women (but mostly women) sort out their finances as they are going through the process of divorce. When a client comes to me, they're fairly certain that something has gone wrong with the money. They suspect there is income they don't know about, money being hidden in a secret account, inappropriate spending, or other valuable assets that secretly exist.

Every case is different, but no matter what the specific concerns are, there are common threads across all of them. Clients come to me experiencing the five secret thieves of divorce. Like Jackie, they feel:

Ashamed
Betrayed
Isolated
Insecure
Overwhelmed

These five thieves steal joy and peace of mind. The divorce process isn't just hard; it's emotionally taxing and expensive. And it's something you never wanted.

As a fraud investigator and forensic accountant, I have a passion for helping men and women who are divorcing to uncover the truth about their money. I want them to be fully informed about exactly what has happened to their money and where it is. Once we know the truth about the money, they can restore their sense of well-being and banish those five thieves for good.

The Thief of Shame

Jackie had no idea the list would be so long when she Googled 'attorneys near me.' She could have called her divorced friend and asked for advice; however, knowing she would have to admit to being a failure sent her back to the search engine—'divorce attorneys near me.'

After seeing a few friends go through the process of divorce, Jackie knew how important it was to talk to an attorney right away. She needed to know exactly what her rights were and what the laws said about situations like hers. She already felt like she was at a disadvantage, and Jackie needed to act fast to be sure that she was on top of it all.

Derrick's announcement caused Jackie to relive so many events of the past eight years. Her husband had been naturally good with numbers, so she trusted him to take care of all their finances. Derrick said not to worry about it. This was easy for him, and she'd always have money to pay for the things their family needed and the extras she wanted for herself and the kids.

There were a few times when Derrick seemed overly sensitive about some money Jackie had spent. It didn't seem like a big deal at the time, and she promised to be more careful in the future. But thinking back on it, maybe Jackie should have paid more attention to him making a fuss over a few hundred dollars spent on some new clothes for herself. Money never seemed tight to her, but once in a while Derrick acted like they couldn't afford anything.

Being hands-off with managing the money suited Jackie just fine. There were plenty of other details to manage in their family: soccer practice schedules, extended family gatherings, and staying on top of doctor appointments and medication schedules for their youngest child. Jackie knew she was good at managing the household and keeping everyone happy and healthy. It was natural for Derrick to manage the money, and his leadership in this part of managing the family was welcome.

Jackie hadn't seen a bank statement since her second child was born. Before that, she looked at them most months. Glancing at the bank and credit card statements and seeing that they had healthy balances in their accounts made her feel like an active part of the money management and gave Jackie a level of comfort.

But when baby number two came, everything seemed so much more hectic. Chasing after a toddler and breastfeeding a newborn took all her energy, and checking up on the finances was an easy task to eliminate. Jackie didn't think about the money details very often because she knew Derrick had it handled. And Derrick was always so good with the money! Unfortunately, her absolute confidence in him left no room for accountability.

What kind of grown woman signs tax returns and other forms without a second glance? What were those other documents I signed last year? A contract? A loan? I know Derrick explained them to me, but where are they? I should probably take a look at them and see what I signed. Why didn't I pay more attention at the time?

For days, Jackie beat herself up for not seeing the signs in her marriage. She blamed herself for not insisting on helping out when Derrick experienced an extremely stressful month a couple of years ago. He was working later nights and seemed so worried about work.

Was he really worried about work, or was he worried that he was going to get caught and his affair would be exposed?

"I could take over paying the household bills for you," Jackie had suggested. She honestly thought if she made sure the utility bills and mortgage got paid and kept the groceries budgeted, it would ease his burden.

"Why? Don't you trust me to take care of you?" Derrick had snapped back at her.

Jackie knew he had worked more than sixty hours that week, so she didn't think anything of it. He was just stressed. But now she questioned her judgment.

I should have asked more questions then.

Dozens of similar scenarios flashed through her mind—like the day she accidentally opened the credit card statement, and Derrick told her she had enough responsibility without worrying about the bank and credit card transactions.

I'm so stupid. How could I not have seen this coming?

The Thief of Betrayal

Within a few days, Jackie found a family law attorney to assist with the divorce. She talked to three attorneys before she made her decision. She walked into each meeting with a list of questions to ask about the divorce process and her rights.

Jackie wanted to know if she would be able to get spousal support and child support from Derrick. She knew that even though they would probably end up with 50/50 legal custody, she'd have more of the responsibility for the kids and she wanted to make sure the finances were fair. And she had left her job to stay home with the babies, so it was going to take some time to get her career going again. Would Derrick have to pay spousal support to help out?

Jackie also asked about the approach each attorney recommended for her case. She wanted to know if she had an attorney who leaned toward fighting or compromising.

In the end, she was most comfortable with Mr. Palmer. He talked about some cases he handled that were similar to hers. He seemed very knowledgeable about the law, but more importantly, she liked the strategy he outlined for her. Mr. Palmer seemed like he wanted to help Jackie have an amicable divorce, but he'd fight for her if it became necessary. And she felt comfortable with him, which was important at a vulnerable time like this.

"We have to start with discovery, Mrs. Carter." The young legal assistant laid a form on the table in front of Jackie. "We need some personal information up here— your name and wedding date. Then down here, you'll need to list your assets and liabilities—things like your house, cars, appliances, loans, and other debts."

Jackie sat there stunned. She knew some of the information, but this form asked for dates and values.

"Are you working anywhere, Mrs. Carter?"

It took a minute for Jackie to swallow the tears so she could speak. "I have an interview at my children's school tomorrow. They need a substitute teacher's aide. Hopefully, they'll hire me. I'm looking into online classes to update my marketing knowledge, but the school position should get me through until I can find a job in my career field."

That was probably more information than he wanted, Jackie thought. When she got nervous, she tended to talk too much.

The legal assistant added a few more forms to her stack. "Fill out as much of this as possible, and when you come in the next time, you'll meet with Mr. Palmer again. Thank you for choosing our firm. We know this is a hard time, and you're trusting us with your case."

Jackie left Mr. Palmer's office with thirty minutes to spare. Not really time to go home before school pickup. As she sat in the school parking lot, waiting for the children to come out, she reclined the seat of the SUV just a bit. She didn't realize she'd dozed off until her phone beeped.

"Hello."

"Hey, babe."

I should have looked at the caller ID before I picked up. "Derrick, I'm not sure I can handle being 'babe' anymore."

"Yeah . . . sorry. Can I come get the rest of my things tomorrow?"

Jackie knew if she said anything, he would hear the tears. The last thing she wanted right now was for him to see her being weak.

"Jackie?"

She swallowed hard. "Yeah. That will be fine. Maybe you can come after the kids get home so they can see you, and you can tell them what's going on?"

"Do you want me to pick them up after school tomorrow?"

Her first thought was *Michaela is in fourth grade, and now you want to start picking them up after school.* But she bit her tongue. "That will be great."

"See you tomorrow, then."

"Yeah, tomorrow."

Drained—how could one simple phone call leave me so drained?

By the time she finished the evening routine with the kids, Jackie knew her mind couldn't handle the legal forms, so she grabbed one of the larger suitcases Derrick always took on business trips. Packing up his clothes would make his visit shorter and keep her busy.

He'd already taken most of his jeans, suits, and underclothes, so she started with the bottom drawer where he kept his off-season clothes. Derrick had always been so good about switching those out so she didn't have to. He could be so considerate sometimes. It would only take a few minutes to pack up the sweaters.

That's weird. Why is one of our Visa statements here?

Her stomach dropped immediately. Jackie didn't want to be one of those paranoid women who was looking for deception everywhere. But it was hard not to be suspicious, knowing that the last three years had all been a lie. And yet, she immediately knew a credit card statement didn't belong under some off-season clothes in a dresser in the bedroom. A drawer Derrick knew Jackie was unlikely to ever look in.

Jackie picked up the envelope and discovered it also contained a variety of stubs and receipts—concert tickets, restaurants he always said were too expensive, and a statement from a bank where they'd never had an account. The credit card statement boasted his favorite football team in the corner. She'd never seen him use a card with that logo.

She had felt betrayed when he told her about the three-year affair, but these papers were all dated five years ago, long before Derrick told her it had started. Jackie was kicking herself for not being more suspicious of the timeline. Don't they always say that a cheating spouse never confesses to all of it?

How much money has Derrick spent on his mistress? Was there only one? Where else has he taken her that he wouldn't take me? That money could be in college funds for our kids instead of being spent on hotels and fancy dinners.

The questions poured into her mind, compounding Jackie's feelings of shame and making her feel even more betrayed by the man she'd given her heart to. It seemed every time she turned around, there were more facts to discover about his love affair and the financial infidelity. The feelings of betrayal sometimes felt so devastating that Jackie found it hard to breathe.

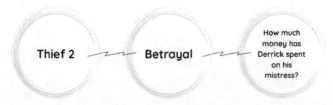

The Thief of Isolation

Everyone knows someone who has gone through divorce. They probably all know multiple people who got divorced. But it still feels so isolating. Women like Jackie often feel like all they see are happy couples everywhere. It was so embarrassing to admit that Derrick was sleeping around on her.

What if friends and family think it's all my fault? I wasn't a good enough wife. I was too focused on the kids. Things weren't spicy enough in the bedroom. People are going to assume the worst, even though I know I was the best wife to him. But maybe . . . .

She did what so many women do to themselves when facing divorce. Jackie started second-guessing herself. Maybe she could have done more to support Derrick's career. Maybe she could have asked him if he needed more from their marriage. Was she somehow missing some of his needs?

Don't do this to yourself. Don't do this to yourself. I can't help it.

Jackie cried herself to sleep every night for two weeks before she could bring herself to tell her mother, sisters, or best friend what was going on. Even then, it was only because Michaela accidentally forced her hand.

"Jackie, Shaniah just told me what happened." It was her friend Lauren on the other end of the phone. "She said Michaela was crying at school and told her about it."

Oh, God. Oh, God. Someone knows. I wasn't ready to tell anyone yet. I look like such a fool. I'm not ready for this.

"Are you alright? You should have called."

"I'm . . ."

What am I? I'm not fine. I don't know what I am.

Jackie was alone. She had isolated herself to avoid embarrassment. Plus, as long as she didn't tell anyone else, she could stay in denial pretending the separation wasn't real until she hit the shower at night and sobbed quietly under the cascade of water.

After a short conversation, with tears making Jackie's words nearly unintelligible, Lauren made an in-person appearance to console her good friend. Unfortunately, without someone to help her walk through the muck of the financial betrayal, Jackie's feeling of being alone could persist.

Telling family and other friends was hard. People were saying they were sorry, and then there was the awkward silence. Jackie knew they wanted details on what went wrong. At first, she wanted to protect her family's privacy.

No need to make Derrick look bad. I'll keep the details to myself.

But not speaking the truth led to further isolation, even when family and friends were showing support. It's hard to cover for someone's bad behavior. They didn't need all the dirty details, but they didn't necessarily need to be denied the truth: Derrick violated his marriage vows. And Jackie finally decided that the best way to not feel so alone was to be honest.

Derrick has been having an affair for several years, and I recently found out.

No one needed to know any details, and they were all polite enough not to ask. Jackie could feel a tiny bit of pressure release. Maybe she didn't have to be completely alone in this process.

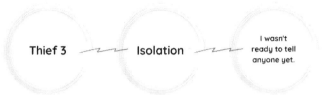

The Thief of Insecurity

After Jackie recovered from the shock of Derrick's admission, she started thinking practically. She and Derrick decided together when Michaela was on the way that she would be a stay-at-home mom. Jackie was five years into her marketing career at the time.

Imagine where I'd be if I had stayed in my job. I'd be an executive by now. Maybe not making as much as Derrick, but close. I'd have my own retirement account too.

But now, she would be responsible for a mortgage, utilities, and groceries in a home by herself. With no job. No career. No source of income. Not to mention all the responsibilities with the kids. The boys had just joined their sister as soccer players, and Michaela needed to be chauffeured to dance classes twice a week too.

Let's just see how often Derrick volunteers to shuttle the kids around. That will still fall on my shoulders.

A part-time job would be easier with the kids' schedules, but would it be enough to pay the bills? Derrick made overtures that Jackie and the kids would be taken care of, but why would she trust him now? The last five years had all been a lie.

I'd be foolish to believe that he'll willingly pay for two households. What happens the first time I don't agree to something he wants? Will he cut us off financially? Will I be able to pay the bills?

When Jackie found out the school needed a mid-year substitute teacher's aide, she jumped at it. It would be something until she figured out a long-term plan. By the time the interview came, she doubted her chances. Her background was in marketing—not that she'd be able to keep up in that field anymore—would they even consider her resume?

Insecurity doesn't only relate to the money. Feeling financially secure is important, and it's one of the bigger issues when going through divorce. But feeling self-worth is a form of security too. Knowing that you have skills and abilities that are in demand is important. Feeling like you can keep a roof over the heads of your children is critical. The process of divorce can break you down and make you question everything. How do I feel confident, capable, and worthy again?

Thief 4 ~~~ Insecurity ~~~ Will I be able to pay the bills?

The Chief of the Thieves: Overwhelm

Even after the school told her she could start as the teacher's aide at the beginning of the next month, Jackie still felt overwhelmed.

Will thirty hours a week be enough?

Can I fill out all those forms the lawyer needs?

Will I be able to be there for the kids emotionally?

Should I take those classes at the college so I can return to marketing after the school year ends?

What will all the other moms think?

It's all too much for me to handle.

The anxious thoughts kept coming. Each time she told herself to stop and just breathe, Jackie would be alright for an hour or so, but then another thought would intrude.

Divorce is a logistical nightmare. The family has to create and adapt to new routines. Schedules are harder to manage when the parents live apart and might disagree about who does what. Attorney meetings, court dates, information gathering, and filling out forms takes hours upon hours. The cost of divorce balloons quickly with the attorneys, experts, and filing fees. Who can keep it all straight?

Jackie knew she needed help, and while she appreciated all the running her mom was doing for her and the lunch dates with Lauren, she realized that she was in over her head. Derrick had been cheating much longer than he'd said, and his infidelity went well past the bedroom. She felt like she was hanging on for dear life.

Thief 5 — Overwhelm — It's all too much for me to handle.

That's Where I Come In

Like many, Jackie felt blindsided when her husband admitted to the affair. She could barely process the information. Cheating was the furthest thing from her mind at that time. She couldn't wrap her arms around the betrayal. This man, who she had been with since college, who she thought she knew everything about, was keeping the biggest secret of his life for years.

> ABOVE ALL, BE THE HEROINE OF YOUR LIFE, NOT THE VICTIM.
>
> —Nora Ephron

Immediately, she started wondering about other things he lied about. Her mind went right to the money.

Oh my god. How much money did he spend on this woman? What if he's hiding money so they can start a new life together?

Jackie had good reason to worry. About thirty percent of relationships experience some kind of financial infidelity.[1] The definition of financial infidelity can be a bit ambiguous, but it generally includes dishonesty about money. It includes things like secret spending, hidden debts, spending money inappropriately, or hiding money. If an action related to the money in your relationship feels dishonest, it's probably financial infidelity.

Finding out about a spouse's affair can be devastating, and discovering your partner has been withholding key information about your finances can be equally damaging. It surprises some when they discover that any deception can be considered financial unfaithfulness.

Ashamed

Betrayed

Isolated

Insecure

Overwhelmed

---

[1]   Harzog, Beverly. "Survey: 30% Have Dealt with Financial Infidelity." *U.S. News and World Report.* Published January 26, 2022. https://money.usnews.com/credit-cards/articles/survey-30-have-either-committed-financial-infidelity-or-been-a-victim.

When I investigate fraud in my role as a forensic accountant, I find things that you might automatically agree are suspect. But I also find things that most people wouldn't notice, even if they are staying active in the management of the finances. Jackie could have missed the signs, even if she had been directly involved in Derrick's money management.

For more than twenty-five years, I've been helping the "Jackies" of the world take control of their divorces, uncover the truth, and come away with their fair share of the money.

PART ONE

FRAUD

CHAPTER ONE

THE FINANCIAL INFIDELITY AVALANCHE

Derrick's Story

It's not unusual for one spouse to have primary responsibility over the finances in the marriage. After all, it's a partnership. You trust one another, and you divide family responsibilities. One person takes care of the yard, while the other does the laundry. One parent drops the kids off at school, and the other one picks them up.

When it comes to the money, most couples find it easiest to have one person manage it. This arrangement is nothing to be ashamed of. It's common for one spouse to know little about what is going on with the money or what the account balances are. You trust your spouse.

The problems begin when one person is intentionally kept in the dark or decides to relinquish control to the point that there is no accountability. When the spouse in charge of the money is operating completely autonomously and with no oversight, the risk of fraud rises.

Had Jackie been more involved in the family finances, she might have seen signs.

It Starts Small

As Jackie discovered, almost five years before they filed for divorce, Derrick had hidden receipts and statements in a dresser drawer she never went into. He knew Jackie would never have reason to look there, so it was the perfect place to hide the evidence.

But the drawer of secret receipts is not where things began. It all started when Jackie quit her job to be a stay-at-home mom.

How lucky that Derrick's job allows me to stay at home and raise my babies, rather than putting them in daycare and missing all the milestones.

While Derrick's income covered all the bills and allowed them to put a substantial amount in savings, they had agreed to tighten their budget on some "extras" when they lost Jackie's income. It was just the safer move to eliminate some unnecessary extravagant expenses. Fancy dinners would be reserved for anniversaries, and neither of them really needed SiriusXM®. But when they talked about canceling all the streaming services and online subscriptions, Derrick felt cheated. He played several games that required a monthly fee. Knowing Jackie would never notice twenty dollars going out of their account each month; he didn't cancel them.

Deep down, he knew if he had mentioned it, Jackie wouldn't have cared all that much. Sure, they were doing some belt-tightening, but Derrick knew his wife.

This type of small expense would not really bother her. Why he hid it, he didn't know. But he did, and that small transaction every month opened the door for the fraud snowball. Little by little, it became easier for Derrick to spend money secretly. It was only fifty dollars here or a hundred dollars there. Jackie would never miss it, and these things made him happy. After all, he was the one going to work every day and bringing home the money.

And the Snowball Grows

Derrick loved technology. His parents had always spoiled him with the latest gaming systems, and he updated both of their phones every time a new model came out. Jackie had come to expect it, even though it was not important to her to have the latest and greatest phone for herself.

Still, because they'd agreed to cut back, when he bought the upgraded model for himself, he made sure the new case was identical to the old one. When Jackie asked if he was going to upgrade, he lied. She didn't care if she had a new one, and he felt guilty getting one for himself without upgrading hers.

But the real test came when Derrick's buddies asked him for his share of their season ticket package for the professional football team. When he and Jackie discussed finances before Michaela was born, that was one of the things Derrick agreed to give up. Let the guys pay for the season ticket package without him, and maybe he'd still be able to attend a game here or there if one of them wasn't able to go to a game. Jackie knew it was a difficult choice for Derrick to back out of the whole package because he loved hanging out with his friends, and live sporting events were his favorite.

"We'll just catch the games in Jim's man cave instead," Derrick conceded.

Unfortunately, he hadn't told his friends, and when the deadline for ordering the tickets came, the fraud snowball grew. Derrick justified it to himself. He couldn't let his friends down, could he? They had done this for years. His share of the ticket package covered four games. It wasn't like he was paying for all of the home games.

Jackie expected him to leave the house to go to Jim's every week. It never crossed her mind that four of the home games were actually trips to the stadium for Derrick. Little did she know that not only was Derrick spending the money on the tickets, but there was also parking, tailgating, and beer during the game. These weren't cheap outings.

He made up excuses on those days to leave the house early. Usually, it was a "home repair" that he was helping with. Derrick was so handy, and he was always willing to help his friends, so Jackie never gave it a second thought.

No Going Back Now

When the season tickets came with an offer to get a credit card with the team logo on it, Derrick jumped on it.

It will make it easier to purchase the tickets and other things that Jackie doesn't need to worry about if I have a card without her name on it. She has enough to do without thinking about finances.

He told himself that he did everything for the family. Derrick convinced himself that he opened a new bank account that only had his name on it for the family. Yes, he believed this was in the best interest of his family. If Derrick put one-third of his pay and his bonuses in this extra account, it could be his fun money. He could make sure the family had what they needed without feeling guilty about indulging his fun side.

This scenario is so common in cases of financial infidelity. The lies grow little by little. There is always a justification for being dishonest about the money. Setting aside money for secret spending is rationalized. The spouse wouldn't understand, shouldn't be burdened with too much information, or simply doesn't need to know. The fraud snowball gets bigger and bigger, but it's often a slow process, so the dishonest spouse doesn't even realize how it's growing.

This is exactly what happened to Derrick. He rationalized every move. He was prepared if Jackie ever found out about the secret bank account and secret credit card. All of the spending could be explained. He could give her his reasoning for everything he did.

Derrick didn't realize at the start that having only his name on these accounts would come in handy two years later when his biggest client asked if he would take her to dinner to continue the meeting.

Jackie didn't think a thing when Derrick sent a text message: *Meeting running over – eat without me.*

A Divided Heart Leads to a Divided Life

Caleb was only six months old when Derrick's relationship with his client turned into something more. He was the project manager, and she was the main point of contact for the client. They always had a good working relationship and got along very well. There was an ease to their conversations, and Derrick couldn't help but compare it to some of the strained conversations with Jackie about the children and the responsibilities around the house.

I never seem to be doing enough for my family, according to Jackie. I'm so tired when I get home, and then she wants me to take over with the kids. She doesn't understand that I need time to just unwind a little after work.

Friendly conversations with the client eventually turned to light flirting. It's harmless, Derrick told himself. But then he went to dinner that evening with her, and things shifted. A second invitation to dinner came the next week. And pretty soon, Derrick was "working late" one or two nights a week. Those dinners with his client were his way to escape reality for a little while.

At least someone finds me interesting. Jackie is always too busy doing something with or for the kids. And when we do have time to talk, all she wants to talk about are the kids. What happened to all the fun things we used to do as a couple?

Derrick believed he truly still loved Jackie, but she didn't have time to give him everything he needed. The lies he told himself had become just as easy as the ones he told her.

I'm providing for the family. I'm doing what I have to do to be successful at work.

He would never admit to himself that these dinners weren't for work. They were completely personal, but they had to fit the narrative Derrick created in his mind.

What started out as one little lie about a twenty-dollar game snowballed and was picking up speed. Derrick played four different online games that each had a monthly fee. Plus, for ten years, he'd been at the football stadium while Jackie thought he was at Jim's. Three phones later, he finally got an upgrade for Jackie at the same time he got himself a new phone. He was certain she hadn't noticed.

Guilt overwhelmed Derrick when Aiden was born, but not enough to stop his deceptive spending. He even convinced Jackie that their growing family meant they couldn't celebrate their anniversary at their favorite upscale restaurant. It wasn't a complete lie. The family bank account had only a little cushion for emergencies.

But the lies about the money didn't stop there. Eventually, the dinners became more frequent. Hotel rooms had to be paid for. Trips out of town were called "business trips," but Derrick was really taking vacations with his girlfriend and paying for them with his secret credit card. He

> "IF YOU'RE NOT HONEST ABOUT YOUR FINANCIAL SITUATION UPFRONT, IT'S LIKELY THAT WHEN THE TRUTH EVENTUALLY COMES OUT, YOUR PARTNER WILL FEEL MISLED."
>
> —Maya Maria Brown, relationship expert

bought her gifts, and those were sometimes expensive. The money spent on the affair was adding up quickly.

Derrick thought he had his double life under control until his top client decided she didn't want to be the other woman anymore. He had to make a decision—return to Jackie, the children, and dreary adult responsibilities or make the fling something more permanent. Derrick knew what he wanted to do, and he convinced himself it was the right thing.

We weren't looking for this. Love found us. We never meant to hurt anyone. But a love like this is so rare. We owe it to ourselves to be happy.

Even the lies about the money weren't really lies and could be justified, Derrick thought. His family had everything they needed and more. He was the one putting in all the long hours and wearing himself out earning a living, and he deserved to treat himself. The money he spent secretly wasn't missed and wouldn't matter in the long run.

Buried Alive and Trying to Breathe

By the time Derrick told Jackie he was leaving, the snowball had become an avalanche destined to bury them alive. The weight of his fraud came crashing down on both of them. There were so many lies. So much money spent on the affair and other things Jackie never would have approved.

As Jackie tried to dig out from the shame of a failed marriage and being totally oblivious to their money situation, Derrick had to face family and friends with some twisted version of the truth. He would never admit to his family that he had cheated on his wife. They didn't need to know.

We are no longer compatible as husband and wife, but we are going to do our best to continue to parent our children together amicably.

Derrick stayed buried under the avalanche much longer than his wife, however. Jackie moved through the stages of grief as she dealt with the emerging truth. Derrick, on the other hand, remained in denial—allowing every financial indiscretion to remain hidden until Jackie or her lawyer confronted him with evidence.

The Reality of Financial Infidelity

Most financial infidelity begins with actions that seem relatively innocent. Hiding receipts doesn't sound like a big deal. Having a streaming account that you don't tell your spouse about could be explained as an oversight. No one wants to be nagged because they signed up for something that costs a measly ten dollars a month.

One survey found that 53% of people in relationships said they had money secrets, but only 27% of the participants believed they had committed financial infidelity.[2] Where is the disconnect in these relationships? Maybe a cheating husband doesn't even realize that he is not just lying to his wife, but he is also lying to himself.

---

[2]   Hecht, Anna. "53% of Americans have kept money secrets from their partner." *CNBC Make It.* Published February 5, 2020. https://www.cnbc.com/2020/02/05/53-percent-of-americans-have-kept-money-secrets-from-their-partner.html.

PART TWO

FRAMEWORK

CHAPTER TWO

PREPARATION

Protecting Yourself Is Like Preparing for War

As Jackie began to work through the papers the legal assistant had given her, the reality of how naïve she had been caught her off guard. She filled in as much information as she could: name, address, e-mail, mobile phone, and details about the family. When it came to the questions about the family finances, it got harder.

She knew they had a checking account and a savings account. Jackie didn't know how much was in either account, but she felt confident that when she got home, she could sign in on the bank's website and see. But where were those investment accounts? A firm that started with an M, Jackie thought.

How silly do I look writing down "M" rather than the actual name of the investment firm? How can I admit I don't know exactly where our investments are? Mr. Palmer is going to think I'm such a fool.

It didn't get any better the further she went on the form. Jackie drew a blank when it came to the questions about car loans and the mortgage. She knew the names of the banks for these, but she had no idea how much they owed.

I knew I didn't know the details, but I didn't think I had to. He kept telling me not to worry about it. He had it under control. How could I have known that I would be filling out divorce papers and need this information?

She thought back to the day she decided to go through the drawers of the desk in the den. Derrick's organization system bewildered Jackie. There was so much information, and it didn't seem all that organized.

How does he keep track of all of it?

Little by little, Jackie found the numbers she needed. However, she also found receipts for items she'd never seen. A new iPad purchased last December? No one in the family had an iPad. An expensive handbag from a department store? Jackie certainly never received that, and she was sure Derrick would never buy a gift like that for his mom or sister.

By the time Jackie got to the back of the desk drawer, she had moved past shock and denial into anger. This had been going on longer than she could have imagined, and he'd been using their family's money to fund his little affair.

Everything they cut back on since Jackie quit her job to stay home and raise the children made her angry now. Jackie gave up the fancy dinners she used to enjoy once a month because it was more important to be a stay-at-home mom. But that money wasn't really saved; it was used to buy the mistress expensive handbags and other gifts. And apparently, there was a secret iPad that Derrick was using!

This is so much bigger than I imagined.

As Jackie was trying to fill out the paperwork the best she could, Mr. Palmer let her know he was ready to see her. She had so many questions. What could she do about all this money spent on Derrick's affair partner? And how could she find out what else he spent or hid? How could she be sure she was getting every penny she deserved in their divorce?

Jackie knew she needed to protect herself and her children, but she had no idea what steps to take. Mr. Palmer previously worked with a forensic accountant, so he had many of the answers Jackie needed.

Plan For Your Divorce

You never wanted to be in the position of getting a divorce. When you said your wedding vows, you believed it was forever. Approximately 700,000 divorces are filed every year in the United States.[3] You have a lot of company in this club no one ever wanted to be in.

There are ways to protect yourself as you navigate the divorce process. And you must remember that you have to look out for yourself first. Your husband isn't going to look out for you. He is going to look out for himself. You need to protect your information, your money, and your children. My expertise is with the first two, so that's where we'll focus.

---

[3] Centers for Disease Control. "National Marriage and Divorce Rate Trends for 2000-2001." https://www.cdc.gov/nchs/data/dvs/marriage-divorce/national-marriage-divorce-rates-00-21.pdf.

Throughout this book, I'm going to provide you with some worksheets and resources that will help you accomplish some of the things I recommend. You'll find these in the Appendix. While the information here may seem overwhelming at times, please understand that we're only scratching the surface on many of the topics. The full "how-to" is found in the online *Divorce Money Guide*,[4] where there are more resources, tutorials, and worksheets to help you uncover the financial secrets being hidden by your spouse.

The first resource you will see in the Appendix is the Planning Checklist. This is a great place to start when you're getting your bearings in the whole divorce process. These items are all about protecting yourself, and we'll see how Jackie used some of these strategies in her situation.

You've Got Mail

One of the first things we need to address deals with e-mail access. Jackie had her own e-mail address, which she frequently used for communications with Derrick as well as all her other personal matters. He didn't have access to log into the account, but he was well aware that she'd had the account for years.

"All right, Mrs. Carter. One of the first things you'll want to do is create a new e-mail address for yourself. Your husband doesn't need to know who you're corresponding with or what you're doing."

---

[4]   *Divorce Money Guide* is available at https://www.fraud-coach.com

"Oh, Derrick doesn't have the password to my e-mail account, so he wouldn't be able to see my e-mails. I mostly use the account to correspond with my family anyway. It's not a big deal."

What Jackie didn't realize is that there was inherently some risk that Derrick could have access to that e-mail account. Maybe she had logged in on the family computer and clicked "remember password," so she didn't have to type it each time. Or maybe she had an old phone in a closet logged into her e-mail account. If Derrick found that phone, turned it on, and connected to Wi-Fi, it might start downloading all of her e-mails.

It is so much safer to create a brand new e-mail account that has never been accessed from any device your husband might have or find. Make the password very secure, and do not include in the password names or numbers he could guess. People tend to use the names of pets or streets they lived on, along with birthdays and anniversaries. Make this password something unique.

It is inconvenient to create a new e-mail address and get things routed to that account. But it's so much safer. You'll be able to communicate with your attorney and other allies confidentially, without any worry that your soon-to-be ex will see the e-mails.

And for the time being, don't allow your computer or phone to remember the password. We don't want your husband peeking when he's visiting the children.

I also recommend that women like Jackie use a different mailing address until after the divorce to keep their spouses from finding anything if they check the mailbox when they visit children or pick up their things. Some use their parents' and siblings' homes, while others rent a post office box.

It might seem secretive or deceptive to reroute your e-mails and snail mail to new addresses. After all, you're used to sharing everything with your husband. Secrets were probably few and far between, at least for you. But sadly, divorce can be like war. And everyone needs to prepare for battle.

You need to protect yourself, first and foremost. Even if you are currently on good terms and have an amicable separation, that is not guaranteed to last. You need to know that your private information is protected. This is the best way.

Most "Jackies" would never have imagined they would need to go to such lengths, but with each secret we uncover, they are grateful they did.

He Doesn't Need to See That

Securing social media accounts is another must-do item on the list. You never know when your social media posts could be used against you, sometimes in the most creative ways. I have seen a husband use a picture of his wife with a glass of wine to argue that she was using alcohol around the children. Fun photographs from a vacation with girlfriends were used to paint her as irresponsible. Photos that included the wife's possessions were used to suggest that she was well-off and didn't need spousal support.

Some of my clients think they can just block their spouse so he can't see their posts, but I recommend limiting social media activity until the divorce is final. Unless Jackie knows and blocks every co-worker, family member, and friend, one of them might show her social media posts to Derrick. He doesn't need to see that.

Jackie discovered the wisdom of this plan when she logged in to change her passwords on her social media accounts. Prior to accessing the *Divorce Money Guide*, she loved posting photos of her children having fun at the park and lunches with her mom friends. Now she realized she was leaving time stamps for her activities and whereabouts. Derrick had hit the like button on every photo and commented on many posts. He even shared them with his friends as if he was still an active participant in the family.

To make it worse, seeing Derrick's social media posts just caused more pain. Jackie didn't want to know he had checked in at a restaurant with his affair partner, and he certainly didn't deserve to know her plans for the evening.

Who would have thought I'd have to be careful about mentioning that I went away for a weekend with my girlfriends?

All this information and the need for change left Jackie overwhelmed and less than confident.

Can I really do this on my own? Derrick always handled my techy stuff.

Bank On It

"Open a bank account at a new bank in your name only."

Jackie felt funny walking into the bank across town. She and Derrick had all their accounts at a bank a few blocks from the house. They had banked there since they moved into the house early in their marriage, and the bank tellers knew them by name.

But, according to the checklist, that was the problem. Since they all knew Derrick, one of them might assume he should have access to information regarding Jackie's personal account. Of course, they legally shouldn't, but after fourteen years of doing everything from a joint account, it would be easy for one of the employees to miss the fact Derrick's name was not on the account.

It is so important to have access to money of your own, just in case your husband drains or closes joint accounts. This is especially true if you are not working and therefore don't have steady money coming in. If you're counting on your husband's paycheck to cover the bills, but he redirects it to an account in his name only, you have a big problem.

Derrick would never do that. Jackie was confident her husband would never take it that far.

But the more she thought about everything she had discovered to date, the more she realized that she needed to be prepared for anything. Jackie never thought Derrick would cheat on her, much less for five years. She never thought he'd spend their family's money foolishly and lie about it. It's not that big of a leap to think that he might cut Jackie off financially and leave her struggling to keep the lights on and put food on the table for their children.

It was time to open that account in her name alone, take some of their joint savings, and put it in that account for safekeeping. Jackie and Mr. Palmer talked about the money Jackie knew about and decided on the right amount for her to move. It was important to Jackie to be above-board in this process, but more importantly, she wanted to make sure she had enough money to make it through this divorce process.

No Credit, No Problem

Jackie continued down the checklist—"Get a credit card in your name."

How will I get a credit card? I don't even have a utility bill in my name. There's no way a bank will issue me a card.

Jackie isn't alone. Many stay-at-home moms think they have very little credit history. But most of the time, their names are on accounts with their husbands. Those joint accounts build the credit of both spouses. While your finances are still intertwined, it is a great time to apply for credit. Even if you do not have a source of income of your own, your household has income, and that will help you get approved.

Fortunately, Derrick had made Jackie an authorized user on all but one of his cards, and her name was on the mortgage. So even though she hadn't worked outside the home for ten years and had only a couple of low-limit cards with her name as the primary, those timely paid joint accounts helped. The trick is to get the card in your name early in the divorce process.

Jackie knew securing her own credit card was just part of facing reality and making life safe for her children.

By the time Jackie made it through the entire Planning Checklist in the *Divorce Money Guide*, she began to feel a bit more confident. She put a lot of time and effort into filling out the papers for the lawyer and taking the steps necessary to protect herself. Hopefully, it wouldn't be a battle, but just in case Derrick decided to make this more difficult, she had a few things in place.

Get Divorced, Not Arrested

As Jackie gathered documents, the bank and credit card statements aroused the thief of betrayal again. The feelings of hurt and anger were sometimes overwhelming. And Jackie wanted to know everything. She felt she needed to know all the details of what happened with the mistress and how much money was spent. It felt like she couldn't close this chapter of her life fully until she knew everything.

He's never bought me anything at the lingerie store. This says he's paying on a life insurance policy. When did that start?

Every time Jackie picked up an unfamiliar receipt, she wanted to know more, so she called her tech-savvy cousin.

"Hey Simon, could you help me?"

"Sure, cuz, what do you need?"

"What would it take to put a tracker on Derrick's car?"

"A tracker?"

"Yeah, something so I could tell where he's going and when he's visiting his girlfriend."

"It's an easy attachment. Where does he park?"

"He's staying in a little apartment about two blocks from your house."

"Perfect. Text me the address."

"Thanks, Simon. Good-b..."

"Wait! Jackie! One more thing."

"Yeah."

"Your name is on that car title, right?"

"No. Does that make a difference?"

"I can't do it then, Jackie. I can't afford to get caught."

"Get caught? It would be on me. You'd only be doing what I'm asking you to do."

"Since you don't own the car, it's technically illegal."

"But we're married. Doesn't that mean it's my car, too?"

"I don't think so. You'd have to ask a lawyer."

"Okay, let me check. I'll call you back if I need you."

Jackie soon confirmed she couldn't legally track the car. In fact, Mr. Palmer told her that she could end up with criminal charges.

She considered hiring a private investigator or having her friend's husband hack into Derrick's computer and add some spyware. That would be a good way to find out if there was any hidden money or anything like that. But the more Jackie thought about it, the less she liked the idea.

> IT'S IMPORTANT THAT YOU DON'T BREAK THE LAW WHEN YOU'RE TRYING TO GET INFORMATION FOR YOUR DIVORCE.

I'm just trying to get a fair divorce, but what would happen to Michaela, Caleb, and Aiden if I ended up in jail? I need to be there for them because, Lord knows, we can't count on Derrick right now.

en she started scheming, Jackie had no idea some of her plans were illegal. Like so many women going through divorce, she just wanted information. She felt like she was left in the dark, and the way to move past the betrayal was to know everything. Jackie didn't consider that knowing all the details might hurt her more, that the details wouldn't truly heal her heart.

If Jackie had been arrested for invading Derrick's privacy or committing computer crimes, the whole ordeal would have been even more devastating for her and her children. It's tempting to want to find evidence of the cheating by any means necessary, but when your divorce is behind you, I want you to come out with your head held high. You can get there!

You'll find even more ways to protect yourself in the *Divorce Money Guide*. I have videos and written materials that guide you through the things you need to do, why they are important, and how to complete them. I want to give you the confidence to make these moves that will secure your information and your finances. Let's continue to walk with Jackie through her divorce process.

CHAPTER THREE

ORIENTATION

Understanding the Divorce Process

Jackie's insecurity and anxiety levels rose every time Mr. Palmer's name popped up on her phone. Was he calling with more bad news? And how much was this phone call going to cost? It seemed every little e-mail or call was costing Jacking $100 or $150. It added up fast, even when she thought she was being as brief as possible.

"Good news, Mrs. Carter, your husband's list of assets and liabilities matches yours almost exactly. That will save us a lot of time."

"I'm not sure that's good news. I know he has at least one credit card that I didn't have on my list. I don't know what's up, but I'd feel more comfortable if I had a few explanations. There has to be a way for us to find out if he has any other accounts anywhere."

"Time is money, Mrs. Carter. We can investigate as much as you like, but I want you to understand how much—"

"I know, Mr. Palmer," Jackie interrupted. "Let me do a bit more digging before we call this finished."

TRACY COENEN

Jackie and Derrick were in the discovery phase of the divorce. During discovery, each side turns over information to the other side. This part of the process includes giving each other documents, answering questions, making disclosures, and possibly even giving testimony under oath with a court reporter present.

Discovery for financial matters can get complicated and sometimes involves lots and lots of paper. It is a necessary process because each side needs to be sure that they understand as much as possible about their financial situation. Jackie and Derrick each had to gather their account statements and complete their lists of assets and liabilities. In more amicable cases, the lists will match, and the process can move forward smoothly.

Unfortunately, too many cases look like Jackie's. In these cases, the lists don't match, or they are missing some important items. How deep the deception goes is anyone's guess, but often a careful look at the account statements you were able to get might reveal clues to the missing items.

Things Don't Add Up

Many times over the next few weeks, Jackie almost told Mr. Palmer to go ahead with what she had turned in. How much would she really be able to get if Derrick had some secret accounts?

What if I spend a lot of money, and then I find nothing? Or what if we find something, but the judge decides there was nothing wrong with what Derrick did? I've heard the courts are biased.

Michaela needed new shoes, Caleb wanted to play baseball, and Aiden had already gone through two pairs of cleats this season. Derrick wasn't really paying his share for all these extras, but Jackie was afraid to rock the boat, so she paid for them herself and did not ask him to contribute. Money was tight even with the child support he was paying and her new job. How would she find more money to pay her attorney? And who would look into the money issues?

Those discrepancies in the bank statements kept nagging at Jackie, though. Derrick's paychecks were usually predictable amounts. Sure, there were a couple of times a year when he got bonuses, and then the deposits were bigger. But twice a month, there should be a standard amount deposited. Except all of a sudden, the deposits were only about half of what they should have been.

Why wasn't I paying attention to this?

They always seemed to have the money they needed, so Jackie didn't have any reason to be suspicious. As far as she knew, they always had plenty of money in their bank account. These statements show they always had at least a few thousand dollars in the checking account. But now it looks like there should have been even more there.

Wait. Didn't Derrick tell me he got a raise a little while ago?

The bank statements didn't reflect Jackie's memory. So, the next time Derrick stopped in to pick up the kids, she asked him about it. But he just brushed her off and called the kids downstairs.

"Let's go get pizza!"

He knew she wouldn't fight with him in front of Michaela and the boys, but Jackie was not willing to let this go so easily.

He may not be willing to talk about it now, but that doesn't mean I have to ignore the issue.

In fact, Derrick's unwillingness to answer her questions made her even more suspicious. Something felt off, and Jackie knew she needed to get to the bottom of it, but she didn't know where to start.

The Process Becomes More Formal

Jackie tried asking Derrick about the finances, hoping they could talk through what was happening. Why involve the lawyers if they didn't need to? But he didn't want to cooperate, so Mr. Palmer said it was time to use more formal methods to get the information Jackie needed.

Each form, e-mail, and phone call added to the expense, and once again, Jackie considered asking Mr. Palmer if they could just come to some kind of agreement to make it all go away. Maybe she'd be leaving some money on the table, but having it over might be worth it. And yet, Jackie knew it wasn't time to let it go yet.

They were still pretty early in the process, and she felt like there was basic information missing from the financial picture. At the very least, she deserved to know what happened to the money. She could decide later if the missing money was worth fighting for. For now, Jackie just needed to get the facts.

Mr. Palmer sent the interrogatories over to Derrick's lawyer, and now he would be forced to answer her questions in a formal way. Derrick saw the list of questions and called Jackie in a rage. How dare she ask all these questions and expect him to give all these details? He took care of the family, and that's what mattered.

Jackie had never heard him so angry before, and this time she only listened for about thirty seconds before she hung up. The fact he blew up like that confirmed Jackie's suspicions. She wondered what he would do when he found out Mr. Palmer sent a subpoena to the bank that issued the credit card with his favorite team's logo on it.

There are several different ways to formally gather information during a divorce case. One way is through interrogatories, which are written questions that must be answered under oath. In other words, there are supposed to be penalties for lying. Your attorney can ask for documents from your husband with a Request for Production of Documents. The lawyers often just send letters or emails back and forth to request documents, but this Request for Production of Documents is a little more formal.

Subpoenas also can be issued to get documents, and in divorce cases, banks are one of the most common places that are sent subpoenas. Mr. Palmer issued subpoenas to Derrick's banks to get statements for the accounts Jackie knew about and to see if there were any other accounts.

When your spouse won't turn over documents you need, it might be tempting to try to break into accounts or computers to get the information. Rather than getting yourself in legal trouble with actions like these, a subpoena can be the tool you need to get the information. Remember, we want to get divorced, not arrested.

Marriage Money Milestones™

Mr. Palmer often asked Jackie to tell him the dates important events happened. Some things were easy—the date they were married, the day they bought their house, and the day Derrick walked out. But there were other important questions Mr. Palmer was asking, and Jackie was having a hard time keeping it all straight.

The Marriage Money Milestones™ worksheet was the secret to organizing Jackie's thoughts and the timeline of major financial events in her life. Jackie finally had a simple way to organize all the information, and she started with the easy things. Next to each event, she wrote down the documents that accompanied the event. For instance, she had the paperwork from closing to go with the date they bought their house.

As Jackie remembered more important events, she put them on the worksheet. She took her time and was surprised when she would remember things. Unloading the dishwasher seemed like a prime time to recall events she had forgotten.

Didn't Derrick's brother borrow two thousand dollars from us a couple of years ago? Did he ever pay us back?

Gradually Jackie added the things that were somewhat related to the initial things she recorded, like the home loan and the time they took a big chunk out of investments to get a new roof. She wrote down the date she quit her job and when they purchased their most recent vehicles.

Creating this time-line for herself brought a lot of tears. Michaela's birthday corresponded with the end of her employment. Derrick's big promotion at work set him up for the "big client" that turned into his affair. Every milestone had a memory associated with it—vacations, family reunions, and laughter.

> NEVER GET SO BUSY MAKING A LIVING THAT YOU FORGET TO MAKE A LIFE.
>
> —Dolly Parton

In addition to taking her on a beautiful (but also painful) walk down memory lane, the Marriage Money Milestones™ worksheet also restored Jackie's confidence; she hadn't been completely oblivious to every financial decision made.

Making a timeline of events is helpful to people going through the process of divorce because it helps them remember important events related to the money. It also helps bring clarity to the dates. You might initially think something happened in one year, but as you add more events to your timeline, you realize you were off by a year. It can also help you remember important money events you had forgotten about, just like Jackie almost forgot about the money Derrick loaned to his brother.

As you go through the divorce process, you will be asked about these important dates many times over. A tool like the Marriage Money Milestones™ worksheet will help keep you organized and accurate. You will easily be able to recall dates and documents that matter by referring back to this sheet. You can find this worksheet in the Appendix.

Financial Disclosure Form

Jackie set aside time every Saturday morning to work on the forms Mr. Palmer gave her. With the new job, other mornings were full of getting herself and the kids out the door, and by the time evening came, she was exhausted.

With coffee in hand, Jackie made her way to the den before the kids woke. Everything from the discovery process was immensely helpful when she got to the Financial Disclosure form. Jackie had already gathered most of the information when the divorce process started. Fortunately, she'd kept a notepad near, so when she thought of something important, she didn't have to worry about forgetting it.

As she filled in the numbers on her Financial Disclosure, Jackie felt a lot better about her situation. She knew exactly what the car payment and mortgage cost each month and had a good idea of their joint investments. The monthly housing expenses worried her, and Derrick's financial disclosure still had a lot of holes, but knowing precisely where she stood with her upcoming expenses eased her fears a bit.

Trust the Process

The divorce process itself can often feel unfair, especially if a divorce is something you never wanted. It's hard to put trust in a legal action that is so painful and one that we have often heard is broken. But the discovery process is there for your benefit, even if it seems long and gets very expensive. Each part of it is designed to provide information so that you and the divorce court judge can make informed decisions.

With this in mind, I want you to use the discovery process to your advantage. Push to get the documents you need, and ask your attorney to send out subpoenas sooner rather than later. Attorneys often want to approach the discovery process informally, making requests to the other side to turn over bank statements and tax returns. If there are delays in providing these documents, it is best to simply send subpoenas to companies. You'll be assured of getting your documents, and it is often much faster than if you wait around for your husband to decide if he wants to be forthcoming in your divorce proceedings.

CHAPTER FOUR

IDENTIFICATION

The Red Flags of Fraud

The further Jackie got from the day Derrick walked out, the more clearly she could see what had been happening. During the first few weeks, her emotions got the best of her. She went back and forth between blaming Derrick to blaming herself. Though she hated the thought of not being as available for her children after she went to work, getting out of the house and having something else to think about all day helped put things in perspective.

Jackie had trusted Derrick implicitly, so even after he admitted to cheating and she found receipt evidence and strange deposits, each betrayal completely blindsided her. With each new suspicion, Jackie told her friends, "Derrick would never do that." She couldn't imagine that the Derrick she had fallen in love with was stealing from her children's future.

Additionally, she had depended on him for everything for so long that she couldn't imagine how she would manage without him. The kids missed him so much; Michaela sat with her and cried at least once a week.

It would be hard, but she'd get through it somehow. She was working through all the emotions. Jackie felt so ashamed that she hadn't seen the signs during her marriage to Derrick. Looking back, it now seemed so obvious. Isn't it often that way? In hindsight, we see that there were signs we could have noticed.

But let's be real. You trusted your husband because that is a core part of being married. And it's rare for someone to go into marriage thinking, "I better be on the lookout for my husband hiding money." Most people don't have direct experience with fraud, so they don't know what to look for anyway.

In my line of work, I deal with red flags of fraud all the time. These are the warning signs, both big and small, that fraud is happening. Think of a red flag as a clue that something is happening, but not necessarily proof just yet. I'm used to seeing these things, but my clients are not, so it's easy for them to overlook them.

Not On Our Best Behavior

Looking back, Jackie could see behavioral red flags of fraud throughout the last several years of their marriage. When they first married, even though Derrick took care of paying bills and managing the finances, they often talked about account balances, insurance, and investments. Derrick asked her opinion about everything important. Even after Michaela and Caleb came along, Derrick would ask her to transfer funds between accounts when he was busy. Jackie felt informed, involved, and knowledgeable.

Jackie tried to remember how far back he had been secretive. Her first recollection was right before they found out Aiden was on the way. Derrick had given her a form to sign while she was feeding Caleb. When she asked what it was, he told her it was just a paper their financial advisor needed for one of their investment accounts. He assured her it was nothing to worry about, just as Michaela tipped over a cup of milk.

She didn't think of this as a secret move at the time. But it seemed unusual, and she could recall it now because Derrick had always given her long explanations before he had her sign things. He was always careful to make sure she understood exactly what she was signing before she signed it. But this was different. He glossed over it and didn't give her any real explanation. And even though Jackie knew this was different, she didn't push the issue.

Why didn't I ask more questions? It wasn't like me to sign something without knowing what it was for.

Jackie kept kicking herself as she recalled the signs she had ignored. She remembered the time she found out Derrick was shopping for a new car, and Jackie knew nothing about it. Would he really have gone through with buying the car without telling her? If she hadn't found out in time, maybe. It bothered her that he was working on such a big transaction and never even discussed it with her.

And there was a time she wanted to log into the bank account online, and Jackie found that the password she had wasn't working. She asked Derrick for the password, and he told her she didn't need to worry about it. He had everything under control. Jackie insisted that she wanted to look at the bank account, and Derrick kept putting off her requests for the password, saying he couldn't remember it. She eventually dropped the issue because it did not seem worth the fight.

It wasn't like me to give up so easily on something important. I guess I just thought other things were more important at the time. I thought it was silly to worry about it.

Derrick had more and more late nights at work every month, and he missed most of Caleb and Aiden's soccer games that season. She believed him when he said he was trying to move up at work and build his bonus so they could take a nice vacation the next summer.

Little by little, Derrick kept things from her, but Jackie had brushed it off as him being sweet as she cared for three small children and then transitioned to soccer mom/homeroom mother. She now knew she should have paid more attention when he started taking more "work" phone calls in private and said they couldn't afford nice dinners out anymore.

I felt like our marriage was changing. I chalked it up to having kids and the added stress at home and work. But the truth is that Derrick was changing.

The behavioral red flags of financial fraud in a marriage are not always like huge flashing billboards. They are often subtle, and many times there may be changes in behavior that happen slowly over time. Jackie's experience is all too common. Small things happened here and there, and over time those things became a little more frequent and a little more concerning. But having no experience with fraud before, Jackie did what most people do in her situation: she came up with explanations for herself and focused instead on her children and household.

Doctoring the Documents

When Jackie looked at the Financial Disclosure Form filled out by Derrick, she had questions. There was the secret credit card she knew about. Derrick didn't know that she knew about it. When she found those documents hidden in the dresser drawer, she quickly took pictures of the card, the statements, the receipts and stubs, and that odd bank statement. Jackie tucked the documents right back in between the off-season clothes and decided not to pack Derrick's clothes after all. He never knew she saw those.

Derrick didn't disclose that credit card or the bank account when he filled out his forms. So naturally, Mr. Palmer asked questions. Derrick came back with vague, odd answers. He still didn't admit to having these other accounts.

Jackie wondered why Mr. Palmer did not just call Derrick out right away, and he assured her it was strategic. "Let's let Derrick say these are all the accounts he has. Then, after he puts the lie on paper and signs it, we move forward with subpoenas to the banks. We'll have proof for the judge that Derrick is dishonest."

In response to some of Jackie's questions about his disclosures, Derrick provided documents with missing pages and smudged numbers. Jackie didn't understand why he was doing this. Derrick was normally so organized, and he'd know that he hadn't turned over all the pages. When Mr. Palmer pointed out all the problems with the documents, Derrick apologized for the mistakes, then delayed things while they waited on updated paperwork.

These documentation red flags added to Jackie's suspicions. Why couldn't Derrick just give them the documents for all the accounts? Why was he refusing to cooperate?

Jackie considered hiring a private investigator, but a friend assured her a forensic accountant would be a better investment. Derrick's continued deception did help her accept the truth, and after a few months of working and gaining confidence in herself, she realized she could manage without him.

Unreconciled Finances

After Jackie found problems with Derrick's payroll deposits on the bank statements, she started to look for other financial red flags. Going through the bank statements for the year before they separated, Jackie noticed Derrick was going to the ATM a lot.

That's weird. We rarely used cash. Derrick was especially against it because he said he'd rather use a debit card, so he had a record of what we spent the money on.

Jackie wondered if he was using cash to pay for his affair. Or maybe he was gambling.

I guess siphoning off part of his paychecks wasn't enough for him. He had to withdraw cash from our joint account too.

What about that loan to Derrick's brother? She kept coming back to that and wondered if the money was really loaned to him or if Derrick just took the money for himself. If Derrick's brother did get the money, when did he repay it? She never heard about any payments, but that didn't mean Derrick's brother didn't repay it. It might just mean Derrick pocketed the money and didn't tell her.

There were too many red flags to ignore. Each document and deception confirmed that the cost of a forensic accountant would be worth it.

How much will it cost me if I don't hire someone to help with this?

Jackie decided she'd rather invest the money in the forensic accountant now than later feel bad about herself for not making sure she had covered every base and won everything she deserved during the divorce. She had one chance to get this right, and her financial security was on the line. Mr. Palmer said she would most likely get half of the equity in the house, half of the retirement account, and half of all the other accounts.

But Jackie was sure there should have been a lot more in the accounts. Didn't she deserve to get half of that money too? Mr. Palmer agreed that if Derrick had hidden money in accounts they could find, she would likely get half of those. And if they could prove how much he spent on his mistress, they could go for half of that too.

There is a lot more money at stake here. I'm not agreeing to anything until I know the truth.

Show Me the Money

It's my job to help women identify every account, including all the places their husbands may be hiding that extra cash or assets. But how do you even know if there is a risk of hidden accounts?

You may have seen some warning signs like the ones Jackie saw, but you are not certain how concerned you should be. What if you're blowing things out of proportion? What if you're just paranoid? My response is: what if you're not? What if you're seeing things that truly are concerning?

One tool I offer is the Red Flag Assessment.[5] It is a free resource on my website to help spouses determine the risk of fraud in their marriage. Not every red flag means there is fraud, and let's face it, when we're hurt, it's easy to make something bigger than it is. But we might also dismiss things that are serious.

The Red Flag Assessment asks a handful of questions about how you and your spouse manage the money in your household and also asks you to identify whether you've seen any

TAKE THE RED FLAG
ASSESSMENT AT
FRAUDCOACH.COM/
REDFLAGS

---

[5]   Access the Red Flag Assessment at https://www.fraud-coach.com/redflags

of a number of potential red flags. After you answer the questions, I'll tell you how likely it is that you have financial fraud in your marriage and give you my recommendations for the next steps.

For those who score high risk, it's time to tell your spouse, "Show me the money." It is important to follow up, dig into the finances, and find out exactly where the money went.

Like Derrick, spouses who commit financial infidelity often create bank accounts in their name only, deposit only a portion of their paycheck, or use cash so their spending can't be tracked. They will hold back information during the divorce, forcing their spouse and lawyers to issue subpoenas, dragging the divorce out for months longer than necessary.

Jackie could have saved herself some grief if she had seen these unusual things during the marriage. She stopped looking at the monthly bank statements, so she didn't even have a chance to notice them. Would she have noticed them if she had been looking at the statements each month? Who knows if they would have jumped out at her or not.

Yet, having both partners involved in the finances on some level just makes sense. Even if one spouse has most of the responsibility, a second set of eyes on the numbers helps keep the other person accountable. As an added benefit, if one spouse becomes ill or incapacitated, the other can easily take over paying the monthly bills.

The movie Jerry Maguire came out in 1996 and quickly became famous for one catchy line. Rod Tidwell is talking to his agent, Jerry Maguire, and telling him that he is going to keep him as his agent. But Jerry has to do just one thing for him: *Show me the money!* He eventually gets Jerry to yell SHOW! ME! THE! MONEY! Over and over. And Tidwell keeps him as his agent.

> SHOW ME THE MONEY
>
> —Rod Tidwell
> to Jerry Maguire

That clip is funny, but I wanted to turn the sentiment into something actionable in divorce cases. A catchy line in an old movie became "find me the money" because I know that if I show women where to look for the money in their divorces, they are capable of finding it.

CHAPTER FIVE

ORGANIZATION

Gather the Statements and Tax Returns

Jackie filled out a number of forms with lists of assets and liabilities and all sorts of other financial information, but now Mr. Palmer wanted account statements. She felt a bit overwhelmed when the legal assistant said he would need statements for the last three years from every account she had in her name as well as their joint accounts.

Mr. Palmer made it clear that this included all the bank accounts, credit cards, investment accounts, and even their retirement accounts.

How many hours is this going to take me?

It was hard not to feel resentful every time something like this came up. Everything in the divorce was costing Jackie time, money, or both. Between the kids, her new job, and trying to take some courses to update her marketing skills, it would be tough to find the time to gather all sorts of account statements.

I never wanted this divorce to start with. How could Derrick do this to me?

Jackie tried to keep it all straight, but it was hard getting involved in the finances so late in the game. Derrick took care of it all. He knew where the accounts were and what credit card companies they used. Whose name was on which account? It was going to take a lot of time to sort it all out.

Make a List and Check It Twice

Jackie looked at the list she had given to Mr. Palmer. They had so many accounts. A few were set up when they first married. One gave them airline points, and another had great cash back. Jackie opened a couple of credit cards at department stores to take advantage of discounts.

To make sure she got all of the accounts, Jackie used the Account List worksheet from the *Divorce Money Guide* to start with. Then as she started gathering the statements, she used the Document Inventory worksheet to make sure she got statements for all the months. You can see both of these worksheets in the Appendix.

Jackie pulled the files from the drawer in the desk and began filling in the blanks: the account name, the bank that held the account, the account number, and the name on it. She was careful to note whose name was on each account. Most of the accounts were held jointly with Derrick, so both their names were on them. A couple of accounts were in her name only, and of course, Derrick knew all about those since he paid the bills.

What about the secret accounts in Derrick's name only? The desk drawer didn't have any documents related to those. But Jackie wanted to be sure that Mr. Palmer knew about them, so she included them on the Account List worksheet. Thanks to the pictures she took of the statements hidden in the dresser drawer, she knew the names of the banks and the account numbers.

When she was done filling out the Account List worksheet with all the account statements she could find, Jackie was troubled that this was probably incomplete. There were some empty file folders in the desk drawer that clearly had papers in them at one time.

Why had Derrick cleaned those out?

Two other things troubled Jackie as she glanced at the statements. One bank statement showed an electronic payment to a credit card company she didn't think they had a card with. She went through all the statements again and didn't see any such credit card there. Jackie added that credit card to her list of accounts, filling in what little information she knew.

Download the Details

The desk in the den only had one big drawer that could have held the account statements and tax returns, so it wasn't hard for Jackie to quickly determine what was there and what was not. The den was not big. There really wasn't anywhere else that papers would have been kept. So, Jackie did some digging. She found one box in the garage that looked promising, but it held forms that were too old to matter.

By the time Jackie tried to log in to get the statements, Derrick had changed the passwords on the bank and credit card accounts. Jackie again thought back to the time she tried to log into the bank account, and Derrick wouldn't give her the password.

Why wasn't I more persistent with it? When did he change these passwords? Was it after we separated, or was it long before that? I wouldn't know because I didn't check. How stupid of me. How am I going to get into these accounts?

Fortunately, every joint account allowed for a separate login for each person whose name was on the account. All Jackie had to do was contact the bank and credit card companies and establish her own access. She'd never seen the need for that before, but Jackie became grateful the bank had this available.

I should have set this up sooner. But I need to stop beating myself up about it. I can't be the only wife who left the family finances to her husband.

After Jackie created her logins with her new e-mail address, she started downloading and printing statements. It took a few Saturdays, but she eventually found every statement she needed. She worked on the Document Inventory for the account statements from the *Divorce Money Guide* to make sure she wasn't missing any months.

How on earth did we end up with four bank accounts and ten credit cards? I knew we had a checking and savings account, and I had two joint credit cards and two department store cards. What was Derrick doing with all these extra accounts?

It felt good to have the Document Inventory completely filled out for the accounts Jackie had access to. But she knew the subpoenas Mr. Palmer sent to the banks and credit card companies would be important. He said those documents would probably arrive within a month or so.

Jackie wasn't prepared for all the charges that showed up on those statements. Derrick acquired six credit cards over the past five years that were only in his name. They documented the affair from its infancy. Seeing those charges was almost as hard as Derrick's initial confession. By the time Jackie organized all the paperwork, her last shred of trust in her husband was gone.

Go To the Source

The final thing Mr. Palmer said Jackie needed was their tax returns for the last three years. An inkling of shame hit her again as she remembered signing those without asking a single question. Derrick always said their taxes were straightforward, and that's the reason why he was able to do them himself online.

But when Jackie went to the desk drawer to find the tax returns—she was sure they were kept there—all she found was an empty file folder. As she guessed, Derrick took those documents when he left. Every missing form and empty folder left her wondering how incompetent he thought she was.

What does he have to hide? What do the tax returns show?

When Jackie asked Derrick to hand over the tax returns, he said he couldn't find them. She knew there was no way he misplaced them, but what could she do about it? She felt stuck without them, but as she worked her way through the *Divorce Money Guide,* she found the answer.

Jackie followed the tutorial for requesting their tax returns on the IRS website and was able to download them in less than ten minutes. With a bit of personal information and her driver's license to verify her identity, everything she needed regarding the taxes was at her fingertips—including copies of letters the IRS had been sending them and amended tax returns she hadn't realized Derrick filed.

Check the Boxes

The *Divorce Money Guide* gave Jackie a variety of resources to help her make sure she didn't miss any paperwork. The Account List worksheet and the Document Inventory worksheets—one to keep track of each monthly statement and another for the tax returns—helped her get organized in a way she didn't know she needed.

I was always pretty organized, but with all of these accounts . . . I don't know how I would have kept them all straight without a simple system like this.

It felt good for Jackie to check off boxes on these worksheets—she was accomplishing things. Plus, she could easily see which documents were missing. Jackie didn't have to retrace her steps to remember which account had a missing statement or which one was missing. It was all right here in front of her.

Jackie saved all the statements and tax returns on her computer as PDFs. She scanned all the paper statements. It would be good to have these documents all in digital format, knowing she could print any of them whenever she needed them. It made it easier to get them over to Mr. Palmer's office too. She took the time to organize the statements in date order because she knew it would help her later when she was going through them in detail.

Most everything was checked off on Jackie's worksheets. After the documents came back from the banks and credit card companies that received subpoenas from Mr. Palmer, everything seemed nearly complete. There were a couple of missing statements, but that looked like it was probably an error, and Mr. Palmer could follow up with the bank to get what was missing.

Stay Organized

Organizing the paperwork can be one of the most arduous tasks in this process. You may need to look in many different places and go to a variety of websites. We sometimes contact tax preparers, and often we stumble upon other accounts the cheating spouse hoped we'd never find.

> ORGANIZING THE PAPERWORK CAN BE ONE OF THE MOST ARDUOUS TASKS IN THIS PROCESS.

This is all a process, and we just work our way through the documents and keep uncovering new information. When we find something new, we follow up on that and make sure we get complete documentation for it. Sometimes we get off on a tangent because we discover something unexpected. But we always come back to our Account List and Document Inventory as our master lists to ensure that we're collecting all of the documents we need.

The *Divorce Money Guide* is one of my most sought-after resources. Divorcing women have found that even when they were involved with the finances, there are still gaps in their knowledge because of a dishonest husband.

The framework in the *Divorce Money Guide* gives them a simple process to follow that helps ensure no stone is left unturned. All of the concepts utilized by Jackie are detailed further in the guide, along with the worksheets in the Appendix and additional worksheets to help sort out other issues. For divorcing women seeking additional support in understanding the details of their financial lives, there are two more levels of support. If you find that doing the numbers on your own is too overwhelming, group coaching or one-on-one support can help you with real-time, personalized guidance throughout your divorce.

CHAPTER SIX

INVESTIGATION

Choose Your Own Adventure

While Mr. Palmer sent subpoenas to Derrick's employer to get his pay history, benefits information, and personnel file, Jackie began her own investigation. She already knew he hadn't been depositing the full amount of his paychecks into their joint checking account. She knew she needed to dig further into the bank statements and the tax returns.

The *Divorce Money Guide* gave Jackie three options for analyzing the numbers in the bank statements and credit card statements, which felt like a "choose your own adventure" to her. She could look at the totals going in and out of the bank accounts to see if the numbers made sense or count up the number of different types of transactions throughout the year. Those two seemed pretty easy, and she was excited to see just how many times Derrick paid their Citibank credit card, especially since she already noticed one month with two payments.

What else is fishy?

The third option seemed more complicated. It would take more time for Jackie to put the numbers from the statements into a spreadsheet, but she felt better about looking very carefully at each and every line item. She had been good with Excel when she worked in marketing, so Jackie was confident she could do this. If she got stuck, she could always call one of her friends who was an accountant.

Each of the three methods of analyzing the bank and credit card statements promised to take her on an adventure of discovery. All would challenge her to investigate further and would be part of the most frustrating part of this entire process. But the worksheets and video tutorials in the *Divorce Money Guide* made it much easier and gave her tips as she searched for clues.

Jackie also found that her work on the spending side of the equation gave her some insight into what she should be budgeting going forward. She never thought much about how much the electric bill was each month, how much they were paying for water each quarter, or how much their monthly mobile phone bill was.

Does the monthly mortgage payment include the real estate taxes or not?

She knew she'd have to look further into some of the items to figure out her budget as a single mom. But Jackie was happy to realize that all this work on the bank and credit card statements was going to give her a lot of information that she could use to come up with her spending plan.

Mr. Palmer filed motions for temporary child support and spousal support, and the following week,

Jackie would find out how much she'd officially receive each month to keep paying the mortgage and feed the kids. Jackie didn't want to file these motions at first. Derrick was paying the mortgage and giving her money, and she did not want to rock the boat.

"Can't we keep this amicable, Mr. Palmer? If Derrick stops paying the mortgage, then maybe we can file these things in court."

Mr. Palmer appreciated Jackie's desire to keep things as friendly as possible. But he explained that these motions were for her protection. "If Derrick stops paying the mortgage or sending you money each month, then we'll have to go file the motions and wait to get a hearing. You could easily go a month or two without money to pay the mortgage while we wait for the court system to address it."

Jackie knew this was not the time to take any chances. Derrick would just have to understand that this is part of the process.

I never wanted a divorce. I didn't cause this situation. I owe it to myself and the kids to protect us as much as possible. Too bad if Derrick's feelings get hurt because I'm getting this stuff formalized so he can't play games.

After the hearing on temporary support, Jackie would know exactly how much she'd receive each month while they were going through the process of divorce. The money Derrick had been giving her really wasn't enough to cover all the household costs and children, so Jackie hoped the judge would agree that her request was fair.

Deeper Dive

The credit card statements gave Jackie more questions than answers. She could account for nearly every expenditure in the last eighteen months; however, when she looked at the statements prior to that, the feeling of being overwhelmed returned. Hundreds of dollars every month were spent at restaurants she'd never been to, and for flowers she'd never seen. Nine hundred dollars in June three years ago went to a hotel on the other side of town, and nearly every month showed at least four hundred dollars with the racetrack as the beneficiary.

What the heck was Derrick doing?

Fortunately, Michaela, Caleb, and Aiden stayed at Jackie's mother's house the night before because when she created the category 'cheating' on her spreadsheet, she needed a half hour to recover.

How could I not have seen this?

I feel so foolish.

How could he do this to me—to us?

But why did that kind of spending stop?

Oh! That must have been when he got that secret credit card.

Jackie thought she'd found most of the indiscretions when she was gathering and organizing the statements, but now that she had time to dive deeper, she found more odd transactions that raised more questions. She wrote down every suspicious expense. The sooner Jackie finished, the sooner she could feel her feelings of betrayal. Right now, she had to focus on the facts, and when she finished the spreadsheet, she would worry about emotions. Every time she thought she'd defeated those thieves, one of them mocked her. And as she went through the rest of the statements, all five thieves reared their heads.

Follow the Flow

The tax returns left Jackie confused. Derrick filed amended returns three times in the past five years; she would need to talk to someone who knew more about these things than she did. Jackie would see if her accountant friend could help with this. On the other hand, the copies of Derrick's W-2s fueled her investigative juices.

Jackie pulled up her checking account spreadsheet for the last calendar year and sorted it by category. They didn't receive the documents from Derrick's employer yet, but in the spreadsheet, all the transactions she believed to be paychecks fell together. Jackie knew these were paychecks based on the dates of the deposits, even though the amounts were always different. Since Derrick worked as a salaried employee with bonuses, they should have all been the same, with a couple of extra deposits a year. She knew there was a problem.

After adding up the twenty-four random numbers on the bank statements, Jackie compared the total to his W-2 from the same period. She knew the W-2 showed his gross income, and she had to subtract the taxes that were paid to get to the "net pay" that should have been deposited. The deposits fell short of Derrick's net pay by nearly $68,000 just for one year.

That can't be right. I must have done the tax part of this wrong.

She did the math again. Gross pay, minus federal taxes withheld, minus state taxes withheld, minus Social Security and Medicare taxes….. the math was right. Wow. $68,000 short for one year was more than $5,000 a month that wasn't accounted for. That explained the low savings account.

The biggest surprise had been the Schedule Cs Derrick filed with their tax return four years in a row. She had no idea he'd been doing consulting work on the side. Two small companies had paid him $20,000 each for his services. Hiding money like this seemed to be a pattern for Derrick. And then Jackie wondered if he had been doing this consulting work on his employer's time—cheating on them too.

Secret Accounts

As you investigate your family's income and spending patterns, the five secret thieves of divorce may resurface. It is difficult to stay calm and joyful when you begin to uncover even more deceit.

The good news is that with every indiscretion you find, you are building your case, increasing your self-confidence, and moving one step closer to finding all the money that belongs to your family. The missing money that Jackie uncovered had to be

> PERHAPS SOMETIMES REMINDING OURSELVES THAT WE DO HAVE A CHOICE MAKES IT EASIER TO PICK THE HARDER ONE.
>
> —Eva Melusine Thieme

somewhere, and since Derrick had already developed a pattern of using secret credit cards, she was going to make sure that her lawyer did everything he could to uncover everything with subpoenas.

You may think you're done finding documents after going through the organization phase; however, in financial infidelity cases, we nearly always find more room for deception during the investigative phase. That may send you back to find more documents. It is a process, and you could find yourself getting more and more account statements.

When my clients go through the *Divorce Money Guide*, they discover several places to look for funds they'd never considered. Most don't think their tax return could give them clues to income outside of paychecks. If Jackie had looked at their tax return before signing it, she might have discovered Derrick's racetrack activities before the divorce. The government requires the casino or racetrack to report that income; a cheating spouse can't avoid putting it on the tax return.

The investigation phase often becomes an adventure because you never know where the money trail will lead. My goal is to put you in charge of your journey using the method that makes the most sense for your situation and timeframe. The investigation part may be the most difficult physically and emotionally, but it's also the most rewarding as we move toward the end of our journey. This is where you really find the money.

CHAPTER SEVEN

POSSESSION

Win What You Deserve

Is it really possible to get what you deserve out of this tangle of lies? After all, that's the point of the whole process, right? You know this will affect the rest of your life as well as the lives of your children. You want to get every penny you deserve in your divorce because you only have one shot to get your share of the assets.

Deserve may not be the exact right word to use. No one deserves to go through a divorce. If you've made it this far, you've already experienced more pain than you deserve and done more work than you deserved to do. No one comes out of a divorce unscathed. However, the work Jackie has done to this point has put her in the best position to avoid feeling cheated one more time . . . when the money and other assets are divided.

Secret Spending

Jackie had already uncovered so much secret spending by Derrick. She'd found evidence of his gambling and taking his affair partner to fancy restaurants. The expensive lingerie and jewelry purchases crushed her, and she had a hard time thinking about all the income from his job that had gone missing.

When she realized the ramifications of Derrick's secrets, Jackie could barely breathe. Even if he'd only been hiding the paycheck fraud for two years, when she included the consulting income, she couldn't believe she had let over $200,000 disappear without questioning it.

But how could I have known?

If one of the stages of grief is anger, Jackie found herself moving through them at a good pace. When she uncovered the first few accounts and receipts, she felt betrayed and depressed. But as she began to think about the kids' college funds and the trip to the Grand Canyon they canceled because the house needed a new roof, her insides boiled.

We would have had plenty of money for all the extras and a bunch in savings if he hadn't been hiding all this money and spending it on his mistress.

Should she keep looking? Jackie felt like she had uncovered so much already. If she kept digging through the statements, she knew she'd probably find more. Even a second look at some of the statements would probably reveal things she hadn't noticed the first time. There were just so many details, and she wasn't a forensic accountant.

And yet, Jackie knew she did good work. She doubted herself at the beginning of this. There were so many documents and so many transactions. But she found it. She discovered lots of money Derrick hid from her, and it didn't take anything complicated to find it. His fraud was there in plain sight. All Jackie needed was for someone to show her how to go about finding it.

It All Counts

A subpoena for Derrick's credit history revealed several credit cards. It even turned up a loan for a car in the girlfriend's name. Jackie's heart broke again when she read the documents Mr. Palmer gave her.

How dare he take out a loan for a car and then put the car in her name!

"Mr. Palmer, what good will all of this information do? This money is gone. I feel like all it's done is make me feel even worse."

"I'm sorry for upsetting you, but I'm going to try to get you part of this money. We call this kind of spending marital waste. Half of that money that Derrick spent or hid was yours. You deserve to get that back."

Jackie's burden lifted just a bit. She had no idea she could ask for half of the money that was gone. "But if he's spent it all, how do we get it back? Isn't it a little late?"

Mr. Palmer explained that he planned to ask the judge to award Jackie extra equity in the house to make up for what Derrick wasted. There was no guarantee that Jackie would get that extra equity, but with the kind of solid evidence she gathered, it was very likely.

Her lawyer also pulled out the information from Derrick's 401(k) and investment accounts. "It looks like he put the majority of these funds in after you quit your job."

"Yes, he got a nice promotion just before we had Michaela. In fact, that's when we decided we could afford to start a family."

Mr. Palmer wrote some numbers on his worksheet.

"Derrick said I couldn't touch his 401(k). He was very clear that it was his because he's the one who put the money in."

"I take it Derrick isn't a lawyer." Mr. Palmer chuckled.

Every spreadsheet and statement sent Mr. Palmer back to his worksheet. He told her that every document would support their requests. By the time Jackie left his office, she felt a lot better about her future. It looked like all her legwork would pay off.

Jackie and Derrick would meet with their attorneys the following week. If she could just make sure she had enough for Michaela to go to college in eight years and the other two shortly after, she would feel like she had accomplished something.

"The more we can work out amicably, the easier it will go in court," Mr. Palmer told her.

Unfortunately, she had no idea what Derrick would do or say. The man she thought she knew had gotten lost some time in the last five years.

Her Fair Share

Mr. Palmer told Jackie most of the assets would be divided equally, except for where they were asking for extra to make up for Derrick's wasteful spending on his mistress. Jackie found out that Derrick's retirement account could be divided, and her share could be rolled over into a retirement account for her. At least she'd have a decent start on saving for retirement. The joint bank and investment accounts would be divided too, and even though Derrick had siphoned off a lot of money, there was still some money in those accounts.

Maybe I'll have enough to pay for marketing classes.

On the downside, Jackie and Derrick would share the debts too. What Jackie really cared about here was that she did not have to pay off the credit cards that Derrick used for his affair. That would just add insult to injury. Mr. Palmer explained that her investigative work on those accounts proved that Derrick spent that money on his affair, and there was a good chance he'd have to pay those debts all on his own.

If Jackie wanted to stay in the family home, she had to be prepared to buy out Derrick's half of the equity in it. But that's where Mr. Palmer reminded her that they'd be asking the judge to award Jackie extra equity in the house to make up for the money Derrick siphoned off and hid or spent on his mistress. If he was successful with this argument, Jackie wouldn't owe Derrick much, and the house would be all hers so long as she could afford the mortgage payment and upkeep.

The meeting with Derrick and his attorney went about as well as she expected. Jackie didn't say a word. Mr. Palmer did a great job presenting her side and defending her position. At first, it looked like Derrick was going to be cooperative, but when Mr. Palmer mentioned Derrick's 401(k) and the bank accounts he had tried to hide, Derrick shut down. His attorney suggested some reasonable compromises for Jackie to consider taking, but her soon-to-be ex-husband wouldn't have any part of it.

After talking through all of the options with the house, Jackie and Derrick agreed to sell the house. They were uncertain exactly how much each one would get, given that Derrick wasn't exactly willing to give up part of his equity to make up for the money Jackie had found. She didn't know if he was in denial about the money or if he was just being selfish.

Mr. Palmer said the judge could make the decision on the equity if Jackie and Derrick couldn't agree. They could list the house now, and if it sold before there was an agreement on the equity split, they could keep the proceeds of the sale in escrow until things were settled.

Derrick said he would take care of getting the house listed with a realtor. But for the first time in their marriage, Jackie stopped him and stood up for herself. "I'll contact the realtor. I can use anyone you like, but I want to be in charge of this part of the process."

As Jackie walked to the car, she held her head a bit higher, realizing that she'd made her first major financial decision since she and Derrick married.

Know Before You Go

Mr. Palmer warned Jackie that things might get ugly. One year ago, she'd have said he was dead wrong. Derrick had always been such a sweet guy, taking care of the family and always putting them first.

But everything had changed. And though the transformation happened right before Jackie's eyes, it had been such a slow progression she hadn't seen it coming—or had she been in denial? It was important for Jackie to face the fact the man she married had departed long ago. Her job now was to keep calm and be satisfied that she had worked hard to make sure she didn't get cheated twice. Jackie and her children deserved some sort of financial security as she left this marriage.

Jackie called the realtor and got the ball rolling on selling their house. Even though she loved their house so much, and it was the only home her children had ever known, she knew it would be a struggle to afford it on her own. Jackie knew she didn't want to cut it close on the budget every month. She wanted to be able to say yes to the extra things her kids would ask for. She wanted to be able to take a vacation once and a while. A new car might be necessary within the next year. Jackie just wasn't willing to sacrifice everything else to keep a house that was too big and required too much maintenance and lawn care.

She felt confident she could find something smaller but lovely with an affordable mortgage. Or maybe she'd even rent a place for a year or two until she figured out how to resume her marketing career. There were enough options in their school district, and Jackie would take her time finding the right place for her little family.

Jackie and Mr. Palmer had one more meeting with Derrick and his lawyer before their court date. They worked out placement for Michaela, Caleb, and Aiden and agreed on dividing a few of the minor items. Derrick made a fuss when Mr. Palmer mentioned her car and some household items she hoped to keep. Jackie compromised on things like which television she would take and how much of the furniture she would keep. But when Derrick tried to convince her that she would have to buy a new car since all the vehicles were in his name, she stood her ground.

When they finally got to their hearing, a lot of unexpected things happened in the courtroom. Mr. Palmer assured her it could have been very different in another jurisdiction. The judge awarded Jackie two-thirds of Derrick's 401(k) and provided for generous child and spousal support. He gave Jackie the extra equity in the house she asked for to make up for what Derrick had siphoned off and spent on his affair.

Everything else was split pretty evenly, although Jackie had decided to give up on a few pieces of furniture in the house because it just wasn't worth the fight anymore. She had what mattered when it came to the kids, the house, and the retirement account. She could always get some furniture.

When she got home that night, Jackie felt a weight lift. The realtor had someone coming to look at the house the next day, so she would tidy up before she got a shower. As she picked up little socks and put a math book in Michaela's bag, she knew the worst day of her life was over. All her hard work had paid off, and though she could have wallowed in the disappointment of the hundreds of thousands of dollars Derrick had stolen over the past five years, she decided to be thankful for the savings she now had and a chance to make a good life for herself and her children.

Yesterday, her mom told her about a cute house in the neighborhood where she'd grown up. Mrs. Finnegan was moving into a senior community. She'd call tomorrow—the first day of her new life.

Jackie did a lot of work in her divorce to figure out what happened to the money rather than hiring an expensive forensic accountant. Some of the work seemed overwhelming, but she found out that it was manageable by breaking everything down into smaller tasks.

> "I'D RATHER REGRET THE THINGS I'VE DONE THAN REGRET THE THINGS I HAVEN'T DONE."
>
> —Lucille Ball

Every hidden account added to the burden of shame and betrayal Jackie carried. Feelings of loneliness and insecurity plague Jackie and hundreds like her every day when they're navigating the divorce process. These are all normal feelings.

Outcomes in divorces can be very different, even when there are similar circumstances. The laws differ a lot from state to state, and judges have a lot of leeway in how they handle things. Even though no one can truly predict what your outcome will be, being prepared is still the best way you can help yourself.

As you move toward the day when a court determines your future, my goal is to make certain we've done everything in our power to give you the best life possible. You may not leave with everything you deserve, but you can leave with no regrets.

PART THREE

FUTURE

CHAPTER EIGHT

MORE THAN THE MONEY

Six months after the divorce was final, Jackie signed for the little house in her mother's neighborhood. Mrs. Finnegan was grateful to have someone from the neighborhood who wanted to move back, and she took Jackie's first offer. The backyard was perfect for three young children, but not so big she wouldn't be able to mow it herself.

Jackie had to hide her laughter when she scolded the boys for visiting Grandma without asking permission on their second day in the new house. She didn't want her kids to become a nuisance, and she didn't want them going without her knowing where they were, but she had to admit, it would be handy being so close as she forged ahead on her own.

Her mother watched the kids on the two evenings she had classes. Jackie had already talked to a marketing firm. They were not scared off by her ten-year absence from the field, and they had a position that would be a great fit for her. It would give her exposure to a variety of projects while she brought her skills up to date. They made her an offer, with the promise of a promotion once she was done with the three courses she needed.

The last twelve months felt like twelve years. Jackie spent so many months in denial and anger, feeling ashamed, insecure, betrayed, isolated, and overwhelmed. But standing here in this house that would belong to only her and would be where she would raise her children, and thinking about the great new job she secured for herself, Jackie realized that the money she found was only a small part of her victory.

I'm happy I fought for what was mine, but it's about way more than the money.

Jackie was feeling good about herself because she'd freed herself from the five secret thieves of divorce. Shame, insecurity, betrayal, loneliness, and overwhelm stole Jackie's joy at the beginning of her divorce journey, and they could have paralyzed her if she had let them. But Jackie did the work, got help from the *Divorce Money Guide*, and ultimately persevered.

From Shame to Pride

Shame overwhelmed her when she realized she had allowed Derrick to keep her in the dark about their finances. For months, Jackie played those scenes over in her mind—all the tax returns and forms she'd blindly signed and the lies she'd believed. She hated to tell anyone about all the hidden accounts and cards, and she started to believe she wasn't smart enough to handle her own finances. The only positive thing about those accounts he put in his name was that they hadn't affected her credit rating.

As Jackie collected the statements and made discoveries that led to finding those accounts, she began to feel better about herself. She remembered how well she'd done in college. She'd always had a little extra in savings and had paid a lot of her student loan before she graduated.

Why did I allow Derrick to make me feel like I couldn't make it on my own?

Jackie's confidence grew with every bill she paid. On the day she got her certifications, Jackie beamed with pride. She was now SEO and Social Media certified. The principal and teachers where she worked as an aide bought a cake and celebrated with her on her last day. The marketing firm came through as promised. She had to start at the bottom, but they assured her they thought she could move up fast.

On top of that, she had been there for the kids' games and homework even while working. One of her biggest fears had been that her job would interfere with what was best for her daughter and sons, but even Michaela seemed to have more pride as she watched her mom work and manage the home on her own.

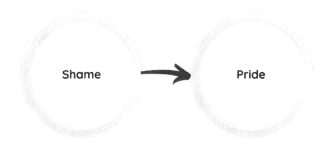

Shame ➡ Pride

From Betrayed to Restored

Every time Jackie found another receipt for a secret expense or hidden account, feelings of betrayal consumed her. She cried herself to sleep on so many occasions that she lost count. Being betrayed by Derrick, her most trusted person, was, at times, overwhelming. For months, Jackie lived in a fog of depression. Caring for Michaela, Caleb, and Aiden kept her going for many days because she knew she had to stay strong for them. But it certainly wasn't easy to be present for them and to put on a good face.

Jackie worked at the marketing firm for about two months when she realized she wasn't living in the shadow of Derrick's betrayal anymore. It had been more than three months since she'd had to face him on the evening he had helped the kids carry in their baseball gear and overnight cases.

"Mom!" Michaela yelled. "We're home."

"No need to yell, Mich . . ." Jackie was a bit surprised when she walked into the living room. "Hi, Derrick."

"Hey, Jackie. How are you doing?"

"I'm good. Thanks for helping the kids bring their stuff in."

As they shared a minute or two of small talk, Jackie realized she felt very little. There was no love, no hate, no anger, and no depression. She recognized that she still felt resentful. After all, he broke up the family Jackie wanted for the rest of her life. They had so much together, and he took it all away and crushed all the dreams she had for the future.

But for the first time in almost two years, she didn't feel like she needed to pull herself together after he left. Derrick had created a huge hole in her heart and self-esteem the day he left, and each sign of betrayal had torn her even further apart, but today she knew the wound had finally healed.

"Caleb, Aiden, one of you should be in the shower," Jackie called as she gathered jackets and bags. Her heart felt light as she climbed the stairs knowing her spirit had been restored. It wasn't easy getting to this place, but it was worth it.

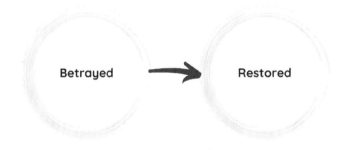

Betrayed ➡ Restored

From Alone to Supported

On the day Derrick broke the news to her, Jackie retreated into herself. Embarrassed that she had let her marriage fail and hesitant to ask for help, she became isolated. Plus, the more

IT WASN'T JUST ABOUT THE MONEY, WAS IT?

—Jerry Maguire to Rod Tidwell

RACY COENEN

proof she found that her husband had been unfaithful with their finances as well as their marriage, the more she tried to keep it a secret from everyone.

Jackie managed to keep everything but their separation from her mother for several months, but when she missed one monthly lunch with her sisters, her mom got worried. Even after Lauren found out about the situation, Jackie avoided her friends for a few weeks, so they got together and "kidnapped" her for an evening out.

When Jackie was at her lowest, those people she shut out rushed in to rescue her.

When Jackie's mom realized she needed to spend Saturday mornings digging through financial records, she offered to let the kids spend Friday nights with Grandma. Jackie's accountant friend gave her a light-hearted scolding when she found out Jackie hadn't called her right away to ask for help exploring her bank statements. And after she realized what was going on, the friend Jackie decided not to call for advice at the very beginning began to check in with her most days. The two got together at least once a week for coffee or to let the kids play together.

"I know this seems hard right now," Jackie's friend confided, "but you're stronger than you think. I never thought I could do this on my own, but here I am, being both mom and dad and doing a really good job at it!"

Jackie had spent so much time taking care of the kids and Derrick that she didn't realize she had also built a strong network of supportive friends, and they all rallied around her once she felt comfortable enough to share her situation with them. Though Jackie would never wish infidelity and divorce on anyone, she knew that without this situation, she would have never known just how great a support system she had.

She started this journey abandoned and alone, but Jackie finished strong and surrounded and supported by important people. Jackie's family and friends stepped up to move her from feeling isolated and alone to being surrounded by people who knew her, believed in her, and supported her.

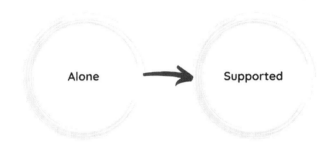

From Insecure to Accomplished

How can I afford to do this on my own? Will Derrick try to take the kids from me? Will I ever be able to get a good job after being out of marketing for so long? How long will I have to work to have enough to retire—I missed ten good years of building my 401(k)?

Those questions and more plagued Jackie at least six months after Derrick walked out. Her mother and father kept telling her they would help her, but Jackie didn't want to depend on them again. The thought of borrowing money from her parents because her husband was a cheater horrified Jackie. And as much as the children loved going to Grandma and Grandpa's house, Jackie didn't want to rely on them for regular childcare. That wasn't their responsibility. Her dad had just retired, and they planned to travel. There was no way she was going to ruin that.

Mr. Palmer had assured Jackie more than once that he expected the judge to award her at least half of those hidden accounts, but she'd been afraid to hold out hope. Everyone says that divorce court is so unpredictable, and sometimes it seems like judges can do whatever they want. Jackie spent months being nervous that Derrick would get to keep all the hidden money and be "Disney Dad" when the kids stayed with him, while she would struggle just to afford the basics.

But the system did not fail Jackie. She got a lot of what she needed and felt was fair. Jackie didn't get everything she believed she was truly entitled to, but Mr. Palmer assured her this was a very good outcome. After the divorce was final and she made her first few mortgage payments, Jackie breathed easier.

The child and spousal support payments helped her get through the first year, but with her previous experience and recent certifications, she quickly moved into a management position at the marketing firm. Now, most of the child support went into a college savings fund, and the spousal support was adjusted to reflect Jackie's higher salary. It didn't really seem fair that Derrick would get to reduce the spousal support he paid after she did all the hard work to "catch up" in the marketing field, but it also made her feel proud to not need that money to keep the household running.

The children's immediate future had been another concern as Jackie embarked on this journey of life as a single mom. All three loved their school, and Jackie was worried she wouldn't find a place to live within their school district. But that was another challenge she tackled, and the kids seemed so happy in their new little house.

One of the first things Jackie did after her promotion was replace her car with a newer model. She didn't necessarily need a new car yet, but there was something about doing this on her own that felt important. When Jackie drove off the lot, she felt successful. For the first time in sixteen years, she had a house and a vehicle in her name alone. And Jackie bought both of those all by herself. She found what she wanted, negotiated the deal, put the money down, and closed the deal.

I did that. Me. By myself.

Jackie was valued and respected at work and was available for Michaela and the boys in the evenings. She worked more than she would have liked, and she had to be creative sometimes to make sure she was free for events at school. And Jackie had to admit that she missed being a stay-at-home mom. It was easier to get them ready in the morning when she wasn't worried about getting herself to work. She liked being able to focus on her family rather than her job. But all in all, she found a way to manage work and motherhood at the same time, and Jackie had a fantastic employer who offered her some flexibility.

She loved seeing Michaela's self-confidence rise with her own. Being the oldest child was tough during the divorce. She tried to protect her brothers and even tried to comfort her mother on more than one occasion when Jackie hadn't been able to hold back the tears. But as Jackie grew in strength, Michaela did too. It was a double blessing.

Jackie felt so insecure when everything started. She'd never dreamed she would have been able to get such a great job so quickly. All the investigation of the finances had paid off. And after all the juggling she'd done preparing for the divorce, she was able to take classes while she worked and took care of the kids. Jackie was proud of her progress and accomplishments.

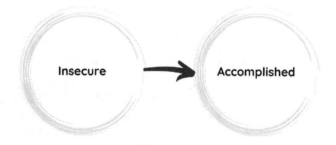

From Overwhelmed to Empowered

Jackie chose to work from home on Michaela's last day of seventh grade. She, Caleb, and Aiden had been through so much. Though Jackie tried to mask her anxiety level, Michaela had asked her more than once, "Are you okay, Mom?" Jackie promised the kids a celebration for the end of the school year this evening.

Michaela shouldered a lot in the last three years. While Jackie packed boxes, her oldest kept the boys entertained. Plus, her daughter even packed up her own room. At first, Jackie felt like she was putting too much on her daughter; however, as she watched Michaela mature and grow into a beautiful teen, she realized the added responsibility had given her confidence. She learned to cook simple meals and helped her brothers with their homework. As Jackie considered the changes in her daughter, she smiled because they mirrored her own.

When Derrick confessed to the affair and said he was leaving the family for the other woman, Jackie felt overwhelmed. She had been so focused on being a wife and mother she began to believe she couldn't do anything else. But as Jackie put the finishing touches on the marketing plan for her client's new product rollout, the confidence she'd developed in the months leading up to her divorce trial resurfaced.

Jackie had come through the most tumultuous time of her life in victory. She was proud of everything she had accomplished. She discovered she had more friends than she imagined, and Jackie knew she had the power to run her own life and succeed on her own.

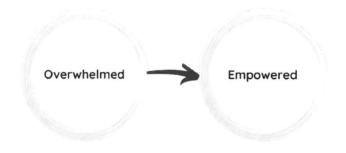

Overwhelmed → Empowered

It's About More Than the Money

> SOME DUDES MIGHT HAVE THE COIN, BUT THEY'LL NEVER HAVE THE KWAN. IT MEANS LOVE, RESPECT, COMMUNITY . . .
>
> —Rod Tidwell
> to Jerry Maguire

Jackie took the Red Flag Assessment on my website when Michaela was just ten years old. It showed her how vulnerable she had left herself when she stopped looking at the family's finances. Before Jackie started following the steps in the *Divorce Money Guide*, those five secret thieves of divorce controlled her emotions and paralyzed her.

But going through the process methodically, little by little, Jackie slowly gained confidence and knowledge. The divorce process stops some people in their tracks. They give up because giving in and over-compromising is sometimes easier than doing the work it takes to make sure you don't get cheated twice. But Jackie and those like her overcome. The reward at the end of their long journey makes every step worth it.

TAKE THE RED FLAG ASSESSMENT AT FRAUDCOACH.COM/ REDFLAGS

It wasn't until Jackie recognized the changes

in herself and her children that she realized the time she invested in winning everything she deserved in her divorce went far beyond the money. Defeating those five secret thieves is an even greater achievement than gathering the paperwork and filling out the forms. No amount of money could trump Jackie's feelings of pride, restoration, support, accomplishment, and empowerment.

Pride

Restored

Supported

Accomplished

Empowered

AFTERWORD

You Are Not Alone

Jackie may be a fictional character, but she represents the one thousand women I help every year with the *Divorce Money Guide.* In Jackie, you'll find characteristics of a variety of the women I meet—and you probably see yourself in many of the situations she encountered with Derrick and her divorce attorney. Each of Jackie's problems is a real one that I have seen time and again, and her feelings mirror those of my clients.

In 2021, the divorce rate increased to 2.5 per every thousand people in the United States. In the same year, there were six marriages per every thousand people. The number of divorces is nearly half of the number of marriages. On average, there are about 700,000 divorces filed every year in the United States.[6]

You can see that there are so many women in the same position as you. They are going through the same

---

[6] Centers for Disease Control. "National Marriage and Divorce Rate Trends for 2000-2001." https://www.cdc.gov/nchs/data/dvs/marriage-divorce/national-marriage-divorce-rates-00-21.pdf.

frustrating process, and most probably never imagined they would be there. But you are more than just a statistic, and I want to walk through this messy time with you.

Many people ask if I created the *Divorce Money Guide* from my experience. Though I have never been divorced, I have helped thousands navigate the system. I estimate that 95% of people involved in a divorce cannot afford a forensic accountant to help them investigate the money, and I knew there had to be a way to help them get to the bottom of their finances.

I don't want to see people like you get shortchanged in the financial part of the divorce. It is not fair that they can't get financial justice simply because they can't afford an expensive expert. And too many times, their lawyers don't know where to look for the hidden money either. All too often, I've heard divorce attorneys say that if you can't afford a forensic accountant, nothing can be done about the possibility of hidden or missing money.

The *Divorce Money Guide* became the answer to the problem I saw so clearly. I knew that if I could create a simple step-by-step process for you to follow, you could do your own investigation into the finances. I thought of it as do-it-yourself forensic accounting without the high price tag. But can you really become a forensic accountant overnight? Of course not. This is why the tools and techniques I give you in the *Divorce Money Guide* are so simple that anyone can follow them.

I give these "Jackies" my heart in this guide because they deserve better than to live the rest of their lives controlled by the five secret thieves of divorce.

No one comes out as the winner in a divorce. Husbands and wives have to learn to navigate life alone, and kids often feel split between the two parents. Worse still, everyone's standard of living goes down after the divorce.

Hopefully, Jackie's story will empower you to surround yourself with those who will support you and give you the courage to pursue everything you deserve so that you can walk into court with your head held high and walk out confident that you have accomplished your goal and are on your way to full restoration.

> FREEING YOURSELF WAS ONE THING, CLAIMING OWNERSHIP OF THAT FREED SELF WAS ANOTHER.
>
> —Toni Morrison

APPENDIX

Find Me The Money

Plan For Your Divorce
Planning Checklist

Use this checklist to make sure you've completed all the steps to
secure your information and your money.

- ☐ Get a new email address

- ☐ Establish service with Dropbox, Box, or Google Drive

- ☐ Open a bank account at a new bank in your name only

- ☐ Open a credit card in your name only

- ☐ Run a credit report on yourself

- ☐ Get a secure mailing address

- ☐ Secure passports

- ☐ Sign out of family electronic devices

- ☐ Log out of shared accounts like Netflix, Hulu, or Amazon

- ☐ Secure all social media accounts

Find Me The Money

The Divorce Process

Marriage Money Milestones™

Date	Events	Documents	Notes

©Tracy Coenen 2023

Find Me The Money

Account Statements
Account List

Type of Account	Bank/Institution	Account #	Name on Account

Find Me The Money

Account Statements

Document Inventory

Year _____

Bank/Institution	Account #	January	February	March	April	May	June	July	August	September	October	November	December

Find Me The Money

Tax Returns

Document Inventory

Year	1040	1120	1120-s	1065
_____	☐	☐	☐	☐
_____	☐	☐	☐	☐
_____	☐	☐	☐	☐
_____	☐	☐	☐	☐
_____	☐	☐	☐	☐
_____	☐	☐	☐	☐
_____	☐	☐	☐	☐
_____	☐	☐	☐	☐
_____	☐	☐	☐	☐
_____	☐	☐	☐	☐

ABOUT THE AUTHOR

Tracy Coenen has risen to the top to become an in-demand forensic accountant for divorce cases and corporate fraud investigations. Her work and her expert opinions have been featured on various media outlets including *CNBC, FOX, ABC, CBS, NBC, Forbes,* and *The Wall Street Journal.* Tracy is passionate about helping women who feel powerless in their financial situations. She created the *Divorce Money Guide* and wrote this book to give women the tools they need to take control of their finances and win the money they deserve in their divorces. Connect at FraudCoach.com

DIVORCE
MONEY GUIDE

Win the Money You Deserve in Your Divorce
Find Your Money and Take Control of Your Finances During Divorce

FRAUDCOACH.COM

DIVORCE
MONEY GUIDE

ONE-ON-ONE HELP

Get Personal Help and Custom
Resources to Help You Conquer
the Financial Part of Your Divorce

FRAUDCOACH.COM

BLOCKCHAIN
VERIFIED IP™

Powered by Easy IP™

Made in the USA
Columbia, SC
17 February 2024

31933285R00072